GO FORTH AND GET A JOB!

A Job Search Guide for College Grads

SULY RIEMAN

WESTBOW
PRESS
A DIVISION OF THOMAS NELSON
& ZONDERVAN

Scripture taken from the King James Version of the Bible.

WestBow Press books may be ordered through booksellers or by contacting:

WestBow Press
A Division of Thomas Nelson & Zondervan
1663 Liberty Drive
Bloomington, IN 47403
www.westbowpress.com
1 (866) 928-1240

Cover photograph by Suly Rieman.

ISBN: 978-1-4908-7321-3 (sc)
ISBN: 978-1-4908-7322-0 (e)

Library of Congress Control Number: 2015904032

Print information available on the last page.

WestBow Press rev. date: 4/13/2015

Suly Rieman

Resume Writing Guide for College Students

Surviving Grief, The Little Guide to Cope with Loss

CONTENTS

DEDICATION

This book is dedicated to my sons, Mitchell and Michael.
You bring much joy to my heart; I love you both very much.
I am so very proud of both of you.
Honor the Lord with your lives and see His blessings flow.

ACKNOWLEDGMENT

Steven P. Schultz, Ph.D.

Steve, thank you for your friendship. Thank you also for your insightful editorial comments. I appreciate your time and kindness to help me with my writing projects in the midst of your own workload and busy life; you are the best!

INTRODUCTION

A Starting Point

Perhaps you are close to graduating from college or you may have recently completed your degree. Are you wondering if you will be able to get a job? You may be burdened with uncertain times, political unrest, a tough economy, and possibly the frustration of not knowing how to get a job. However, you are not alone. Many new college graduates face the fear of the uncertainty of not knowing if they will get a job, where the jobs are, and how to get past the cold and impersonal online job application.

You may think that getting through college was difficult enough for you, and now attempting to find a job to cover the cost of your student loans may seem overwhelming. The same way that college is not for the faint-hearted, neither is searching for a job. I am a firm believer that searching for a full-time job is a full-time job since it involves much more than just submitting an online job application.

Throughout my diverse career, I have had some exciting and interesting positions: project manager, sales manager, hiring manager, professional résumé writer, career coach, and a consultant. I also had the privilege to teach a career development class to undergraduate college students. I understand the time and preparation it takes to be a proactive and be a successful job seeker. I understand the time investment required to build and benefit from a network of friends, family, and acquaintances, as well as to how effectively market oneself. I am honored to have successfully helped many of my clients market themselves, interview well, and get hired.

I wrote this book in hopes of helping college graduates, including my own children, prepare for their job search and plan for their interviews. It is amazing that my children are now young men paving a way in life for themselves. I was diligent to pass along my faith and to teach my children morals. I taught them how to be good citizens, and especially, good cooks. I also decided to take every opportunity to pass along to them the successful tips and advice I have shared with many others in hopes that they, too, will be successful with their post-college job search. Both my sons decided to pursue a college degree in conservative fields: one in business and the other in networks systems administration. Therefore, this guide is written for individuals in conservative or traditional degree programs; thus the conservative job seeker.

This guide does not promise that you will get hired if you follow five, seven or ten easy steps. You may easily lose count of the steps, and find that some steps may be challenging. Getting ready for the hiring process takes time, preparation, dedication, and a strategic plan. I believe it is important to highlight the key and important tasks in the process, so I have streamlined the information. I refrained from including unrelated information or fluff to create a huge book. This quick and easy reference guide helps you focus on the key and important steps in your search.

I wish you the very best as you prepare to find a job and begin your career. Congratulations on your wonderful achievement of completing your degree.

CHAPTER ONE

Job Search Documents:
The Cover Letter

There are three job search documents for job seekers to use: a cover letter, a résumé, and a thank you card. Like with everything in life, opinions vary regarding the use and structure of each one; however, all of my clients have been successful with these black and white recommendations. This chapter discusses the cover letter, its purpose and the structure. Chapter Two, covers the résumé, and Chapter Three, covers the thank you letter.

As a hiring manager, I have seen a wide range of cover letters; some good, and some, not so much. Writing an effective cover letter requires that you research the company and the job for which you are applying. This takes time; however, if you want to be viewed or considered a serious candidate, it is well worth the time and effort you invest.

Purpose

The purpose of the cover letter is two-fold:

1. To make a great first impression on the recruiter or hiring manager as you introduce yourself.
2. You want to secure an interview.

As a hiring manager, I can tell you that if I am not impressed with your cover letter, I assume that I will not be impressed with your résumé. Therefore, it is very important for the candidate to have a cover letter that quickly makes a positive impression on the mind of the reader and guides or frames how your résumé will read. This is an important letter, it must be well written and error-free.

Here are the things to include in the letter:

1. Address the letter to somebody
2. Knowledge of the company and what drew you to apply for the position
3. Tell them what skills you bring based on the job description
4. Ask for the interview

> *The cover letter that includes the personalized details of the receiver sets you, the potential candidate above the competition.*

Dear Someone

Address the letter to somebody requires research to inquire who will receive the letter, it may be a recruiter or the actual hiring manger. Stay away from using archaic catch phrases such as *Dear Sir/Madam* or *To Whom It May Concern*, because frankly, it may not concern anyone! It should not be a shot in the dark. It concerns a real person with an actual name. When I receive a cover letter addressed like this, it indicates that the candidate was not concerned about making a great first impression and was not proactive in finding my contact information. (Your mother would call this lazy!) Sometimes, the name of the Human Resources Manager is listed on the company website; sometimes, the name of the recruiter is listed within the job description. When this information is not listed anywhere, it is time for you to pick up the phone, call the company and obtain the name of the person, their title, and the correct spelling. Use these personalized details to address the letter. When the recruiter is a woman, use Dear Ms. or Miss, along with her last name, since you most likely will not know her marital status. A word of caution, when it comes to names, do not assume the person's gender. Names such as Carol, Kim, Chris, Dawn, Alex, Sam, Evelyn, Michael, and many others are all names of both men and women, so verify this information before addressing and sending your letter.

The cover letter that includes the personalized details of the receiver sets you, the potential candidate above the competition. Also, the name of the recruiter or the hiring manager also provides you with the information you need to search for information about the individual. You can search social media and networking sites to see what information is available about the person. This may help you write a creative cover letter or help you engage in a better or detailed conversation about the company and their position during the interview. Be cautious, and never discuss any of their personal information, such as family, friends or pets when you meet them! You want to make a positive impression and not make them feel uncomfortable or wonder if you are their next stalker.

As you search organizations for the name of the contact, be it the recruiter or the hiring manager, you will find that there may be some organizations that will not share this information. Government offices may not aware that there is a box, let alone think outside of it, so do not be surprised if short of interrogating you, they will not disclose any information. Do not worry or panic, if you know someone at the organization, ask them or simply address the letter to the departmental title, such as Dear Hiring Manager, Dear Human Resources Manager. One other option is to avoid the title by providing a subject line: Applicant for Entry-level Accountant. Keep in mind, these type of offices also may not accept a follow up call and you may need to rely on your personal network to access this type of information.

Knowledge of the Company

Knowledge of the company may be information that you obtained from your research, the experience you gained from an internship or volunteer work, the relationship you may have with a current or past employee, or the reputation of the company. When applying to a company that you know nothing about other than what is in the job description, it is vital that you do some research about them, their products and services. Do not ever attempt to bluff your way through this step: do your research. Visit their company website; find articles about them through the various library and online resources such as *Google Alerts*. Yes, this may take some time; however, if you are invited to an interview, you may be asked what you know about the company. Without some type of research to support your response, you will make a negative impression. I have interviewed several candidates that could not effectively respond to the question: *Tell me what you know about our company*. Regardless of their skillset, they did not receive a job offer. Since they knew nothing about the organization, how could they know if they would want to work there or be happy in the organization?

Tell Them What You Offer

Be sure you read the entire job description and that your cover letter demonstrates that you know the type of skills they seek in a candidate. Employers are great about providing the details of the job requirements, or tell us what candidate must possess, so, it is no secret. They know exactly what they are looking for in a candidate, and as a potential interview candidate, you need to know as well.

Tell them what you would bring to the position means that you actually possess the skillset listed in their job description! Review the key points of the job description, and in your letter relate how your skills match the skills they require. If you do not possess the skills, do not fabricate or lie to make it seem as if you have these skills, because you will not be able to support your statements with specific examples in an interview.

Be sure that you highlight the skills you possess that match their job description. For example, this will aid you in being clear as to why you decided to apply for the position and how you are truly a good match for the position. Do not repeat everything that you list within your résumé, but rather select the key skills they want in the candidate and match them to your skillset.

Ask For the Interview

Asking for the interview may be the most challenging part of the letter for some college students. Most standard letter writing books or websites will tell you to simply say something like, *I look forward to hearing from you soon.* This statement means nothing to a recruiter or hiring manager, and frankly, when is soon? Instead, let the recruiter know that you will contact them to follow-up within a specific time frame. Be certain to keep your word and follow-up with them within the stated time. This is also a good reason to have the name of the person that will receive your letter; you will have a contact to inquire on the status of your application. Be creative and put it in your own words. Ask for the interview. This is why you applied to the position!

Be sure to close the letter with words such as respectfully or sincerely and then your signature. You may create an electronic signature or simply type your name, and submit the job applications over the Internet.

Letter Format

The format of the letter should be a standard one-inch margin, no crayon (a candidate actually submitted a letter by mail written in crayon once). Be sure to type the letter. Be sure to include your contact information, their contact information, and the letter should only be about one half to three quarters of a page long; you do not want to overwhelm or bore the reader.

Things to keep in mind as you create a cover letter:

- Do not mass produce the letter; it must be individualized for each position
- Address the letter to someone
- Be creative and unique to arouse interest in the candidate by the recruiter: do not be silly, flippant or outrageous
- Write concise, detailed, and error-free statements about yourself to make a great impression
- Include the knowledge of the company
- Briefly explain what you have to offer based on the job description
- Request an interview

Do I Really Need A Letter?

Do you need to include a cover letter with every job application? Yes, unless the online application system does not allow a space for it; however, some online applications provide sufficient space to include a brief letter within the résumé box. Also, some hiring managers will not review résumés without a cover letter. In some industries, such as creative arts or video game programming, they may laugh at you for sending a letter that no one will ever read. These industries may strictly hire on talent and no cover letter may be necessary. However, why take a chance? As the candidate, unless you know the hiring manager and their preference, you may take a risk of not having your résumé read if you do not include a letter. Some companies use an online applicant tracking system that does not allow a space for a letter; in this case, you will not need a letter unless you choose to place it with your résumé, or in the blank area of additional skills, or in the box they provide for you to tell them any else they need to know about you.

An Example Letter

Here is an example of a cover letter that includes the key points that address the letter to a specific person, demonstrates knowledge of the company, and how the skills that match the job description, and asks for the interview. Be sure to use this as a guide rather than a template. Strong candidates create interesting letters using their own words (not mine... since that is still called plagiarism!).

As you can see from the example letter, the candidate was brief and yet covered the important sections of the letter without fluff statements. Be sure that your letter is specific to the company and specific to the job for which you apply.

July 20, 2015

10413 North Granite Avenue
Bedrock, AZ 85302

Mr. Jon Smith
Plant Manager
Springfield Power Commission
Springfield, AZ 85336

Dear Mr. Smith,

Please accept this letter and my attached résumé as my application for the Modeling and Simulations Systems Engineer position. From my research, I understand that Springfield Power Commission has been rated one of the top companies to work for in Arizona based on the training and support it provides its employees. I would be proud to work for such an organization and use the training I receive to promote excellent service to internal and external customers.

In June, I received my Bachelor of Science degree in Computer Information Systems from Big State University. In addition to my degree, I have three years' experience with various software products that I used in school and during an internship. Your job description indicates that you seek a candidate with management and configuration of small office networks, and I have two years' experience in configuring and maintaining systems I obtained while working part-time for a local organization.

I will be happy to contact you next week to confirm that you received my résumé and application, as well as inquire about next steps. I am very interested in the position and would be honored to be invited for an interview. I look forward to speaking with you next week.

Respectfully,

Wrigley C. Whitepaw

wcwhitepaw@freemail.net
480 555.2734

Caution!

Do not create one letter and assume that you can use it for every job application by merely interchanging the company information. It is very easy to make the error of submitting the letter with the incorrect company name or values. I once received a letter from a potential candidate that was correctly addressed to me, as the hiring manager and my organization. In the body of the letter, however, she went on and on about all the reasons she would want to work at one of our competitors. Clearly, this was the letter she originally used for her job application with the other organization and she merely forgot to update the body of the letter before applying new. Needless to say, I did not contact her for an interview. Many in hiring positions have had the same experience.

You want to make a great first impression on your potential new boss, so take the time to create a great letter to make a great impression. Be sure that their contact information is correct and the body of the letter is clear that you are applying for a position within the correct organization.

CHAPTER TWO

Job Search Documents: The Résumé

If you were to speak to ten résumé writers, you may get ten different opinions on your résumé; however, as a professional résumé writer, hiring manager, career coach, I understand what all résumés need to do: create a résumé that will wow an employer within a very short time. Most recruiters and hiring managers spend anywhere from five to ten seconds glancing at a résumé, before deciding to read it thoroughly. This means that your résumé must make a positive impression in this short time in hopes that someone will read it to consider inviting you for an interview.

Sections

So, let's talk about things to include in your résumé. The sections or the headers to include are your contact information, education, associations, certifications, projects, and work experience. Depending on the degree that you earned, you might include a skills section or details about your core major courses, internships, externships, clinical or medical practicums, or rotations, volunteer work. All or some of these sections may need to be included in order for your résumé to be up to industry standards. Try to stay away from templates and cookie-cutter résumés; I rather have a résumé tailored to the industry standard and current to meet the needs of the hiring manager. By industry standards I mean, a résumé for an engineer should not look like a résumé for a video game programmer or an art major. Each style must focus on things that are relative for the degree and should be current with the industry needs: this information may not be readily available to job seekers, and this is one reason a guide such as this is helpful! I speak with recruiters and other résumé writers and discuss successful trends. The résumé should be relative and current and not include things that are no longer being used, such as, *references available upon request*, at the bottom of the document. Also, I highly recommend that a new college graduate have a one page résumé since it is difficult to wow an employer with a multi-page résumé, full of fluff and lacking the specifics of someone already with years of work experience and special projects. A one page résumé is easy to hand out at career fairs, interviews, networking events; it ports well over the Internet and, like a business card, can easily be given out to anyone that you meet!

Contact Information

Your contact information should include your name, mailing address, phone number, and email address. If you would like to maintain some privacy, you may list only your city and state if that makes you feel more comfortable than listing your full address. You may consider omitting your address if you plan to apply for a position outside your local area and not be easily weeded out due to your geographical area. However, you will be required to provide your complete address on job applications.

Your email address must be a personal email rather than your school email. If you have a school-issued email, your school may discontinue this perk within a few weeks of graduation, and you do not want to miss notices from employers. Use a personal email name that an employer can easily identify, such as your name or your first initial and last name separated with a period or an underscore symbol. Stay away from using tags your friends may find amusing but can damage your chances of getting an interview, such as hothoe@, sexyboy@, crazyjoe@, methking@, or ikillforfun@, and so forth. You will definitely make an impression on the hiring manager, however, just not the impression you need to be granted an interview! Create a dedicated email for your job search, and you will have better control on receiving and replying to employer inquiries.

If you list two phone numbers, such as a home landline and a mobile, then indicate which one is the home number and which line is the mobile phone number. When you list only one number there is no need to identify the type, simply list the number.

I Object To the Objective Statement

Objective statements are now antiquated and not recommended. If you do not plan on using a cover letter, then you may consider including a short, two to three sentence summary in your résumé. If you decide to place an objective statement in your résumé, be sure that it is clear and concise and does not contain fluff statements, such as: *To obtain a challenging position as a cost accountant in the manufacturing industry with a growth-oriented firm with an opportunity for advancement.* No kidding – who would not want that? Simply state your objective: *To obtain a career as a cost accountant.* If you write the objective statement based on a specific company or specific job opportunity, then make sure to update the objective statement the next time you use your résumé for another job title or company. This is the main reason, it is unwise for you to use a one-size fits all objective section or statement.

Education

For most new college graduates, work experience (their part-time jobs helping pay for school), may not be relative to the degree they just earned. Your education may be the strongest marketable skill that you possess, so list your education as the first section after your contact information. You will want to list the full name of your degree along with the month and year that you completed your program. Then list the name of the college with the city and state. If you completed your degree through an online program, then list the city and state of the school's corporate address rather than your local state, or simply do not list any location information. If you have a grade point average, GPA of 3.0 and above, then include it. Below 3.0 will not distinguish your credentials from other candidates. If you achieved dean's list or president's list, then be sure to include those honors. If you have other college degrees other than the one that you just completed, then include those. And be sure to list your degrees in reverse chronological order: The degree you just completed is the most relevant.

If your degree is not easily understood or easily recognized, such as technical management, which has nothing to do with technology, then you may want to include the high level course work for your program to clarify your major. Do not include your lower level courses or your general education courses; only list the high level, program specific classes. When the job requirements indicate a knowledge of math or science for example, then add the hours you have for those courses.

Do not list your high school education on your résumé. Since you completed your college degree, it is safe to assume that you completed your high school requirements. The only exception for listing your high school information would be, if from your research you find that the human resources manager or hiring manager went to the same school! Be sure to remove it from the résumé for the next job application.

Skills

If you chose to create a skills section, then include three to six skills that are relative to your program or degree or that you can tie to the prospective position. Avoid listing things as detailed oriented unless you can provide specific examples to back up the generality. If you place excellent communication skills on your résumé, be prepared to showcase that skill during your interview. Be honest with everything you place on your résumé and be prepared to support it in an interview. Avoid irony and humor within your skills section, and avoid the mistake others have made by listing *fire breathing, scapegoat, housebroken, leader of a 5,000 member clan in a video game,* or *most talented individual.*

Experience

If you had the opportunity to participate in an internship, externship, medical clinical rotations or practicums, be sure to include it. You may include the title you held, the department, the class it pertained to within your program, the tenure or time frame you were there, the hours you earned, and the name of the company with the city and state. Then list two or three achievements, not tasks or duties of your work.

Senior Capstone Project

If you developed a project or completed a senior level or capstone project be sure to include it in your résumé, especially when the senior project relates to the position for which you hope to apply. Talk about what you did on the project to showcase your skills and then talk about what the project entailed. If you earned special recognition or an award for your project, do not be shy, include it.

This is especially important when your capstone projects relates to the type of position you seek. For example, if you plan to work in social or community-related positions and your capstone project entailed specific research or community education, you will want to showcase it. You or your interviewer will want to use these as a talking points in the interview.

Volunteer Experience

Volunteer work may be considered experience when it relates to the degree program or if you are entering an industry, as many boast today, that highly regard giving back to the community, such as social work, healthcare or faith-based fields. List the name of the organizations and your tenure. If you have room within your one page document, briefly describe the type of work you did for each organization. Use this experience as talking points during the interview. Prepare for this by looking at the organization websites to see if your volunteer experience relates to their charitable or community work.

Certifications and Associations

Certifications may also increase your marketable skills when the industry promotes it or the industry requires it. The health care industry and technical industries value certifications, and sometimes the salary range for positions are greater for individuals with the certifications. Include professional associations, such as honor society or that relate to your degree are good to include. Activity outside of school is valuable to some hiring managers, so be sure to include your membership to organizations that relate to your field. List any leadership positions you held with each organization. In your research, you may be pleasantly surprise to learn that the recruiter or hiring manager is a member of the same organizations.

Work Experience

Your work experience does not need to include every job you ever held in life. Your résumé is a highlight of your skills and accomplishments; it is not your auto-biography or obituary. If you have room on your résumé for one or two jobs and still stay within a one page limit, then include them. If you only have room for one job, then include only one job. Be sure to list your title with your tenure and the company with the city and state.

This section is a good place to include your military experience. List your current or last rank, your full tenure, the branch of service and you may list the last place where you were stationed or tour of duty. Accomplishments such as awards, letters of recommendation, medals, and honorable discharge are a good way to showcase your service.

Accomplishments, Not Tasks

You may only have sufficient space to list two accomplishments – not tasks, not job descriptions, not the things you were responsible for, but accomplishments. As a hiring manager, I am not interested in what your responsibilities or job duties were; I am interested to see what you accomplished within the job. What difference did you make within the position?

For example, if you served coffee at the local coffee shop, you took orders, made coffee, and helped customers. This may be true and self-evident; however, this merely showcases that you showed up for work. An accomplishment would be *created a positive shopping experience for customers or provided excellent customer service by engaging with every customer.* See the difference? You are promoting the skills you used to accomplish the task. So think of things that you accomplished at your job and be certain to put it in your own words! Start with the verb and showcase your skills and the results.

To aid you with this task, here is a writing exercise: brainstorm and list all your job duties. Select the key priorities and write clear sentences that will help you showcase your skills and accomplishments. The few examples here show the difference in writing a clear accomplishment sentence and a general task list.

See how this example quantifies the accomplishment by including numbers and quantities to bring clarity to the accomplishment.

Unclear: Scheduled baseball games for the Parks Department.

Clear: Scheduled 40 baseball games monthly for the Parks Department that included hiring 10 umpires and creating special tournament brackets.

This example qualifies your accomplishment: use adverbs to describe how a duty was accomplished.

Unclear: Prepared bank deposits.

Clear: Accurately prepared daily bank deposits within a 0.5% error rate.

Use active voice for your current job accomplishments.

Unclear: Data entry, check verification and order processing for the Accounting Department.

Clear: Accurately enter data, verify monthly checks; process document orders for the Accounting department.

Use past tense for previous jobs.

Unclear: Check account status for customers.

Clear: Courteously served customers, researched accounts, and verified account status; resolved discrepancies. Politely addressed and resolved customer concerns.

Focus on the results.

Unclear: Reorganized filing system.

Clear: Created and implemented an account filing system which eliminated duplication and automated access to complete customer information from one day to ten minutes.

Résumé Styles

There are three basic résumé styles: reverse chronological, functional, and the combination of the two styles. The reverse chronological résumé accounts for the experience and work history in reverse order: your most current job is listed first followed by your previous job. Your current degree is listed first followed by previous degrees or other education. The functional résumé showcases your accomplishments by key areas of expertise, regardless of where you obtained the experience. The combination résumé may be used to list your degrees in reverse chronological order and then account for your experience by accomplishments, and then list the names of the organizations where you worked.

For a recent college graduate with little to no work experience, the reverse chronological style works well. If you have many years of work experience and returned to school to obtain a degree, then the functional résumé may work best for you. You can easily list your accomplishments within your key skill sets or areas of expertise regardless of where you gained the experience. This will also help keep you from repeating similar accomplishments within jobs that you held within the same industry. Examples of each résumé style are included within the résumé sample section.

A *curriculum vitae* or CV is Latin, for *the course of one's life*. A CV is an additional résumé style typically used within the scientific and academic fields in the United States and is commonly used internationally. In addition to education and work experience, the CV allows an individual to list training, research and publications, and it may be more than two pages. This guide does not discuss the details of the CV or provide an example since this type of résumé is not commonly used for entry level, new grad applications in the U. S.

Résumé Tips

Nothing needs to be in bold face fonts within a résumé. The overuse of bold text is similar to sending a note in all capital letters, so avoid using bold text. Since the résumé is all about you, there is no need to use personal pronouns such as I, my, or me. When using bullet points for your accomplishments, avoid long, run-on sentences; keep it brief. Bullet points work well when listing your job accomplishments. Structure the bullet points as you would an outline, that is, if you list one point under a heading, then you will need at least two points. You will want to list only two to four accomplishments per job.

Here is an example:

Barista, October 2012 - Current   Big Cup Coffee House, Phoenix, AZ

- Create a pleasant, engaging experience for every customer
- Provide creative resolutions for customer conflict and concerns
- Recipient of Employee of the Month, three consecutive times

> *Managers would much rather receive great résumés that reflect the people behind the documents.*

Be sure your résumé is typed, well written, and error-free. You do not need to spend a lot of money on special résumé paper as it is acceptable to use standard copy paper. Standard white paper works fine for interviews, and if you decide to use colored paper, research shows that very soft, pale colors or light pastel colors make it easier to read the text. Bold or crazy colors such as glow-in-the-dark green are distracting and often annoying.

Always have your list of references with you and available as you give out your résumé; however, never list the names of your references on your résumé; providing references is assumed and you will include that information within the job application. So, there is no need to place a redundant, antiquated statement at the bottom of your résumé stating that you will provide them upon request; this is no longer used in any industry.

Have plenty of copies of your résumé in your portfolio and always take more copies than you think you will need to your interviews. You may have an appointment with me and I may lead you to a conference room where you will meet three or four other individuals for a panel interview. So be prepared to offer everyone your résumé. What is a portfolio you ask? It is a professional-looking leather or leather-like folder that contains a writing tablet or a large, leather, flat case to carry and showcase artwork. One thing I will say about portfolios, you do not need to spend a lot of money to purchase a leather one when one that looks like leather fits your budget better! (I discuss the details of a job seeker portfolio in chapter four.)

Does All This Make A Difference?

You may wonder if having a great résumé makes a difference from having a good résumé or even a bad one. Yes, there are many cases where an awful résumé nonetheless lead to an interview. But let me give you a few examples about how recruiters or hiring managers decide to filter through résumés.

A well-known medical and service company placed an open position for a new college graduate program on their website and received over 700 résumés. Two recruiters had the task of reviewing résumés and finding 50 qualified candidates for the hiring managers. The recruiters decided to split the pile of résumés between them. After they each took time to filter through all the résumés, they each had selected 100 candidates. They met to review and discuss the résumés and they selected the final 50 candidates to contact for the interviews. The great résumés made it through the final decision stage and those candidates were interviewed and extended job offers. The good and the awful résumés were filed away. My client's résumé made it to the final cut and she was extended an invitation to interview. She received the job offer for her dream job.

I once had an open position to fill and I received about 20 résumés from the recruiter. It was her job to screen the résumés and she selected the résumés that she assumed I would want to see. Most of these did not have consistent formatting, contained errors and featured too many different fonts. Most of them were two pages long, although they did not have sufficient experience to fill one page, let alone two. I wondered about the quality of the résumés she denied! After glancing at the résumés, I made three piles: the read pile, the maybe pile, and the no-way pile. After reading a few résumés, I found the two or three candidates to interview. None of the candidates fully met the position requirements, and I reposted the position.

So, yes, sometimes hiring managers are faced with reviewing awful résumés and even interviewing those candidates; however, no hiring manager simply wants to settle for a body to fill a position. Managers would much rather receive great résumés that reflect the people behind the documents. As a candidate, I would dread knowing that the hiring manager settled or lowered their expectation or standard to accept my résumé, invite me for an interview, and offer me a position. Yes, I would be happy for the job offer; however, I would not like knowing I was at the bottom of the barrel of their choices!

Example Résumés

The examples that follow are simply that, examples. These are meant to be used as guidelines rather than templates. Be sure that everything you include in your résumé is truthful and be sure to put everything in your own words!

Reverse Chronological

Jared M. Phillips

P.O. Box 3972
Phoenix, AZ 85332

602 807.9234
jm.phillps@freemail.net

Software Experience

MS-Word 2010/2013
MS-Office Outlook

MS-Excel 2010/2013
Quick Books Pro 2013

MS-PowerPoint 2010/2013
Windows NT

Education

Bachelor of Science in Business Administration; Emphasis in Accounting
Big State University

December 2014
Phoenix, AZ

Course Emphasis

Operation Strategy
Business Policy

Project Management
Accounts Receivable

Legal Environment
Accounts Payable

Experience

Office Manager
Better Tile Inc.

September 2005 to Present
Phoenix, AZ

- Effectively manage Accounts Receivable and Accounts Payable
- Carefully oversee petty cash and budget and process office supply expense accounts
- Accurately reconcile bank balance, record general debits and credits entries
- Establish customer credit lines and set-up credit accounts with vendors
- Maintain excellent customer relations and developed customer rapport

Assistance Manager
Big Box Electronics

May 2001 to August 2005
Phoenix, AZ

- Directed recruitment and retention of supervising and staff of 45 employees
- Trained employees; effectively supervised and regularly evaluated staff and provided guidance
- Successfully achieved all work objectives
- Successfully implemented and maintained new merchandising projects
- Accurately reconciled all cash transactions that were turned in at end of each day

No work experience to list; includes course emphasis and senior project

Peter N. Abrams
pnabrams@freemail.net
775 982.7986

Education

Associate of Applied Science in Electronic and Computer Design   October 2014
Big State University   Phoenix, Arizona

Course Emphasis

Technical Math	Schematic Reading
LAN Technology	Cicso Networking
Systems Analysis	AC/DC Applications
Electronic Devices	Microprocessors
Physics	Digital Conversions

Software and Hardware Skills

MS Word	Oscilloscope	Circuit Maker	Electron Workbench
MS Excel	RouterSim	Visio Studio	Multimeter
MS PowerPoint	MaxPlus	Switches	Windows NT

Senior Capstone Project

Designed and implemented a demo version of a LAN and WAN network for Sunset Elementary School. Used Cisco Networking Academy technology to ensure successful design structure. Researched compatible hardware and software, selected Windows 2000 to run as the operating system for the networks. Designed the district's server functions with operable software. Created and maintained a cost data sheet for the project and completed project within budget.

Includes senior project and work experience

Ted E. Roosevelt

1121 First Avenue

Phoenix, AZ 85008

212 954.7113

ted.roosevelt@freemail.net

Skills

Excellent verbal and written communication: wrote market studies and presented in meetings

Motivated: worked full time while attended college

Project management: managed six high-level customer projects

Sales and marketing: increased sales by business development strategies

Results driven: meet or exceeded sales goals by 10%

Negotiation: contract processed and executed prior to start date

Education

Bachelor of Science in Business Administration; Emphasis in Marketing

Big University

June 2014

Phoenix, AZ

Associate of Applied Science in Marketing

Small Community College

March 2005

Phoenix, AZ

Senior Project

Created a marketing plan and a business plan for a local pest control company. Developed promotional items for business; created a new logo for the materials. Provided owner with solutions for account and billing issues and created an automated mobile billing systems which decreased process and payment time. Led a team of three in meeting deadlines and completed project within budget. Awarded the Dean's Choice Award for project presentation and documentation.

Experience

Account Executive

Pershing Incorporated

June 2000 to Present

Phoenix, AZ

Respond to customer needs and inquires in a courteous and timely manner. Provide excellent account support and maintenance, as supported by customer feedback. Calmly resolve customer issues and concerns. Increased district sales 25% per year for three consecutive years.

Sales Associate

Big Box Sales

October 1998- May 2000

Phoenix, AZ

Successfully assisted customers with purchase decisions in various retail departments. Quickly addressed and resolved customer issues. Consistently exceeded sales quota; earned employee of the month award.

Functional: Denotes experience by area of expertise

Jonathan M. Doha
john.doha@freemail.net

19858 N. Villas Road
Chandler, AZ 85225

Home Phone: 480 250-1111
Mobile Phone: 623 962-8412

EXPERIENCE

ACCOUNTING

- Research and update payment status on 52 accounts
- Resolve issues with rejected invoices
- Code and process invoices within 24 hours
- Prepare, generate, and review reports on a weekly basis
- Initiate weekly check run and assist in daily, weekly, and monthly reconciliation
- Conduct special financial reconciliation projects

LEASE ADMINISTRATION

- Provide professional technical leasing support for assigned regions
- Create, maintain, review database files
- Establish initial rental payments
- Compile and assemble relevant data for managers, team, and landlords
- Process, maintain, and troubleshoot all market property rental lease agreements, invoices, check requests

CUSTOMER SERVICE

- Respond to inbound communications within 2 hours and in a courteous manner
- Assist customers, dealers, and retailers in acquiring missing parts and literature
- Track and locate shipping information
- Resolve issues for unsatisfied customers in a calm manner
- Create and send quotes to customers within 2-3 hours
- Assist in planning corporate and team meetings
- Provide excellent daily internal and external support

SUPERVISION

- Promoted to Customer Service Supervisor and supervise six employees
- Train new employees and subcontractors on policies, procedures, and resolving customer issues

EMPLOYMENT

Accounting Clerk	Electronic World	October 2007-October 2008
Lease Administrator	Countryside Loans	April 2006-September 2007
Accounting Clerk	Guide Electronics	June 2005-April 2006
Lease Administrator	One Cell	March 2003-June 2005

EDUCATION

Bachelor of Science in Business Management; Emphasis in Accounting, Big University, Phoenix, AZ   GPA 4.0

Associate of Arts, Small Community College, Phoenix, AZ   GPA 3.35

CHAPTER THREE

Job Search Documents: The Thank You Card

The thank you card is a great tool when used correctly. It shows the hiring manager that you are polite, and that you take initiative. It shows them that you are capable of following up with them, and possibly on their projects should they hire you. Best of all, you may use it to remind the hiring manager why you are the best candidate. The hiring manager may meet with many potential new hires and your thank you card may be the very thing that helps separate you from the rest of the pack.

When I interview candidates for a position and have the last two or three candidates narrowed down, the person who sends me a thank you card or letter helps me with my decision. The thank you card or letter may be the thing that closes the sale for you.

A Card

A simple, hand-written card works well. Be sure to thank them for whatever you are grateful for such as their time, their consideration. I always like to thank people for the opportunity to meet them. One major key to this note: keep it real; be sincere! This is not the time to add fluff or inappropriate comments or statements and ruin your chances of getting a job offer. If you do not have legible penmanship, type your note so that the reader can actually understand what you are saying and not wonder what you scribbled.

Sending a thank you letter via email may not be the best option, especially if you have never exchanged email with the hiring manager. Your note may hit their junk mail box folder and they may never see it or know that you sent it.

> *The thank you card or letter may be the thing that closes the sale for you.*

When and Where To Send

Be sure to send the thank you card within 24 hours of the interview, so have a small supply of simple, blank, thank you cards and postage stamps on hand during your job search. You want to continue to make a great impression, and sending the thank you card out immediately will help you with that process.

Hopefully, you have the contact information or asked for the business card of the hiring manager you met during the interview and can correctly address the thank you card. If you do not have their contact information or forgot to collect a business card at the interview, then pick up the phone and call them to find out.

CHAPTER FOUR

The Portfolio

A nicely prepared portfolio will assist you in your interviews and to apply for jobs at any time. A portfolio may be leather or look like leather; no one needs to know you did not spend a lot of money for it! Your portfolio should contain all the relative documents that will help you be organized during the process and allow you to have all the things that you need at your fingertips. For graduates in the field of arts, your portfolio will be the support or proof of the quality of your work, and I will assume you know that you will need to include your work samples. An artist, photographer or architect's portfolio may not be the standard eight by thirteen inch size since your work samples may include large photographs, schematics or pieces of artwork.

> *Have your portfolio prepared for every interview. You will also be ready for the times you might interview for a job that you have not officially applied for yet. This does happen!*

Items to Include

So what should you place in a standard portfolio? Good question – some of the items will be universal for any college major; some items will only pertain to certain majors. Here is a general list of the items you may need:

Résumé Support

- Transcripts or a student progress report

- Copy of your diploma or degree
- Letters of recommendation
- List of three personal and three professional references with contact information
- Copy of your certifications

Related Work Experience and Volunteerism

- List of your work history including company contact information
- Detailed summary of internship, clinical rotations, clinical practicum skills and achievements
- Work samples
- A well-written research paper to support your written communication skills
- Community service projects, senior projects or capstone project information
- Detailed listing of your volunteer work

Background Documentation

- Residence history
- Finger print or clearance information
- Right-to-work documents: passport, social security card, driver's license
- Vaccination verification for international positions, health or social work

Interview Preparation

- List of questions you will ask during your interview
- The job description you will discuss during your interview
- The company research or company information you obtained
- Copies of your résumé
- Paper, pen or pencil
- A calculator
- Your business card

Have your portfolio prepared for every interview. You will also be ready for the times you might interview for a job that you have not officially applied. This does happen! If you are asked to apply for the position, you will be completely prepared to fill out or complete the job application with all the relative information contained in your portfolio. You will feel confident knowing that you have all the necessary information at your fingertips and have impressed the hiring manager with your foresight.

One of my clients took my advice and included a well-written research paper in their portfolio to support her writing skills. She received a high letter grade from the instructor for the assignment. During the interview, the hiring manager told her he thought she was articulate and asked how she could support her excellent writing skills she had listed on her résumé. She was confident as she told him that she had a research paper in her portfolio for him to keep and read to support that very question. The great thing for her, he hired her on the spot!

Letters of Recommendation

Be sure that you obtain three letters of recommendation from anyone that can speak about your work ethic. Instructors, professors, supervisors, co-workers, volunteer coordinators, pastors, clinical or medical practicum preceptors are all good examples of anyone that you may contact for a letter. Avoid waiting until the day before your interview to request a letter. Be polite with your request and allow the individual sufficient time to create the letter and submit it to the organization as well as provide you with copies for your portfolio. You may also help them and remind them of the work you did for them. Send them a draft to fill the details, and also provide them with the date you need them to complete the request.

References

First, ask permission to use the individual's name and contact information. Do not use anyone that has not authorized the use of their information! You may not receive the glowing recommendation you desire. Second, create a list of personal and professional references separate from your résumé. Never include references on your résumé, unless the employer requests the information as one document. You do not want to assume that your references will be contacted, so it is best to wait for the employer to request your references, and be prepared to include your references on the job application.

Prepare a list of three professional (supervisors, professors) and three personal references. Your references should include anyone that can speak to your work ethic. Keep your reference sheet in your portfolio. You may need the list when the employer requests it or to complete a job application after an interview.

Some of you may be wondering, should I include my parents as references? I will say no, unless, you worked for them in their business. If so, you may include them as your boss; however, ask them to keep the conversation on a professional basis. This is not the time to share baby stories; regardless of how cute you were.

Here is an example of the information you would want to include in your references sheet.

Your name

Name
Title/Company
Relationship
Length of time known
Phone Number, including area code or an extension
(Indicate home/work when both are used)
Email address

The Business Card

You may consider creating your own business card to help you as you market yourself. Several companies listed in the Internet offer quality business cards for free with a nominal shipping fee. Inexpensive or free computer programs are also available to create and print business cards on card stock with standard printers.

The business card may contain your name, your degree or major, your email address, phone number, the link to your website or work samples. You may also list key skills, job interest or anything that you believe would help market you and your new degree. You may include a photograph, a graphic design or a work sample that relates to your major. Keep it simple, elegant, and professional. Use your business card at networking events, career fairs, and hand one to the hiring manager when you first meet them or as you prepare to exit the interview: this makes a good impression of you as a serious candidate.

CHAPTER FIVE

Research

I am a firm believer that a good candidate must have knowledge about the organization where they plan to interview. Be sure to research the company before you apply to a position. Sometimes, hiring managers will ask the question: *Tell me what you know about our organization* or *why did you apply to our company*? If you are not aware of what the company does or the products or services they offer, it will be difficult and possibly foolish to reply to this question.

Say What?

I recall the story a hiring manager once shared. He interviewed a candidate and was so impressed with her skills that during the interview he considered extending an offer to her. Before he did, he wanted to ensure she would be a good fit for his organization. After their meeting, he decided to show her around the office and introduce her to some of his employees. To his dismay, during that conversation, she raised the question, "*So, what do you guys do here?*" She did not know what products or services this company marketed. Needless to say, she did not receive the job offer. Do not let this happen to you; take the necessary time to research the companies where you consider applying. Ask yourself why you want to work for them. You want to make a positive impression on the recruiter or hiring manager and show them that you know something about the company and how you fit this position and organization.

> *In addition to the company website, there are some great research tools available to equip you to find valuable information on the company, their location, and recent articles.*

Be in the Know

Before you attend an interview, review the basic company information to enable you to reply to questions or help formulate questions to ask during the interview. Run an Internet search by company or division name: the organization may be part of a larger organization. Visit their website and review the list of products or services they offer, review their vision, mission statement; read about their management and leadership, their community involvement, and their economic status. Find recent articles about them and see what others say about them as well as their overall industry. This may confirm your interest in the company or it may completely change your mind.

You may also be interested to know the cost of living for the city where the company is located and what the rate of unemployment is for the area. Who are their top two or three competitors, and what is the job growth rate for the area? These factors may influence your decision to accept a job since you will want to afford to live comfortably while you work for the organization.

Resources

In addition to the company website, there are some great research tools available to equip you to find valuable information on the company, their location, and recent articles. I have listed a few here for you. Some sites may require that you have a membership to view the information; however, most universities offer these sites to students and alumni through their library resources, so be sure to utilize them, especially those you may use without having to pay a fee.

ReferenceUSA: www.referenceusa.com

Plunkett Research: www.plunkettresearch.com

LexisNexis: www.lexisnexis.com

EBSCO Business Searching Interface: www.ebscohost.com

Bureau of Labor Statistics: www.bls.gov

City Comparison Guide through Sperling's Best Places: www.bestplaces.net

US Census Bureau: Community Economic Development HotReport: http://thedataweb.rm.census.gov

CHAPTER SIX

The Job Application

There is one basic difference between a job application and a résumé - the job application is legal and binding. When you complete job applications, you are asked to confirm and agree that everything you included is truthful, and then you are required to sign it. That signature is like our affirmation, our stamp of approval, and we are held liable when we are not truthful. Everything contained in our résumés must also be truthful; however, legally, we do not need to include within that document everything we have ever done. The résumé is a marketing tool used to showcase our skills, education, experience, and accomplishments. The job application usually asks for greater detailed information about our skills and our work experience, and will be verified by the organizations interested in hiring us. Be sure that you are truthful and complete the document to the best of your ability since the employer will verify the information at the time of a job offer.

Disclosure

Most job applications are similar when it comes to asking basic questions to obtain information about candidates. Few companies continue to use paper job applications. Most use an electronic applicant tracking system, (ATS) that helps screen, eliminate and narrow the number of people in the candidate pool. Be certain to answer every question honestly to avoid getting discredited and weeded out of the process.

Some applications may ask that you list every job you have ever held; some only ask about the last three jobs or the jobs you held within the last ten years. Usually, all job applications ask about education, work experience, military service, and criminal backgrounds. Be sure to reply honestly to all questions. Most employers want to collect demographic information about candidates such as race, gender, disabilities, and so forth; responding to these questions may be voluntary and optional.

Sample Application

As an instructor, I created a student assignment that included a hiring packet. They had to create job search documents for a specific job that they intended to apply. They were to complete a simple job application that I created. I wanted them to get into the habit of thoroughly completing a job application and have this information at their fingertips when applying for actual positions.

After completing this assignment, a student mentioned that he decided to include his completed job application in his portfolio so he would have the information readily available as he networked and applied to jobs. I thought this was a brilliant idea: he streamlined the need for various documents in his portfolio and he could easily apply to jobs at any time.

> *There is one basic difference between a job application and a résumé - the job application is legal and binding.*

APPLICATION FOR EMPLOYMENT

We consider applicants for all positions without regard to race, color, religion, sex, national origin, age, martial or veteran status, the presence of a non-job related medical condition or handicap, or any other legally protected status. Proof of citizenship or immigration status will be requested upon employment.

Date:

Desired Position: Desired Salary:

First, Middle and Last Name:

Address:

Telephone Number:

Have you been convicted of a felony within the past 7 years? __Yes __No
Conviction will not necessarily disqualify an applicant from employment.

If Yes, briefly explain:

Do you have the legal right to work in the United States?   Yes   No

Have you ever been in the military?   Yes   No

Are you willing to take a drug test?   Yes   No

State any additional information you feel may be helpful to us in considering your application: specialized training; skills; apprenticeships; honors received; professional, trade, business, or civic organizations or activities; job-related military training or experience; foreign language abilities.

Work History

List the last three jobs that you held; starting with the most current:

Title: Date employment began and ended:

Company Name:

Company Address:

Company Phone Number:

Supervisor's Name:

Salary: Reason for leaving:

May we contact this employer?   Yes   No

Title: Date employment began and ended:

Company Name:

Company Address:

Company Phone Number:

Supervisor's Name:

Salary: Reason for leaving

May we contact this employer?   Yes   No

Title: Date employment began and ended:

Company Name:

Company Address:

Company Phone Number:

Supervisor's Name:

Salary: Reason for leaving:

May we contact this employer?   Yes   No

Education

High School Name, City and State:

Did you graduate?   Yes   No   or   Earned GED

College or University Name, City and State:

Degree Earned: Year of completion:

Did you graduate?   Yes   No

Other:

Applicant's Statement

I certify that all the information I have given on this application is true and complete to the best of my knowledge. I authorize this employer to investigate of all statements contained in this application, and understand that any false or misleading information I have given in my application or interview(s) may result in discharge. I understand and acknowledge that, unless otherwise defined by applicable law, any employment relationship with this organization is "at will"; this means that I may resign at any time and the employer may discharge me at any time with or without cause. I further understand that this "at will" employment relationship may not be changed orally, by any written document, or by conduct, unless such change is specifically acknowledged in writing by an authorized executive of the organization.

_____   _____
Signature   Date

CHAPTER SEVEN

Dress to Impress

The best rule of thumb for dressing for an interview is to dress conservatively and professionally. Dress to make a positive impression with everyone you meet during the interview. Dress professionally to present yourself as someone that is serious about the interview, very interested in the job, and someone that is promotable. Be sure that your outfit is clean, pressed, fits comfortably, free of the smell of stale body odor, cigarette smoke, alcohol (or puke) and ready several days before your interview. Give yourself sufficient time to get your outfit professionally cleaned and back home days before your interview appointment.

Do not concern yourself with what the average employee wears at the company where you have your interview. The employees may wear whatever they want that adheres to the company policy because they work there…you do not. Dress one step up from them for the interview and always dress one level up from the job for which you are discussing. Meaning, if you inquired about the dress code and the hiring manager lets you know that their policy is business casual, you may still consider wearing a suit for the interview. Also, for medical professionals, the job may require a uniform; however, for the interview dress professionally. Do not show up for the interview appointment a medical uniform.

> *The best rule of thumb for dressing for an interview is to dress conservatively and professionally.*

The Business Suit

A business suit works well for men and women. A suit wears well, looks professional, and indicates that the candidate is serious about the interview. A grey or navy blue suit is best for day time interviews. For men, a black suit works well for a wedding, funeral, or social evening events, not for interviews. For women, a black suit is acceptable for an interview, be it a skirt or pant suit. No need to spend a lot of money to look great: never pay full retail price! I have purchased some beautiful suits at re-sale shops and from the clearance racks. Keep an eye on the local sales, use coupons, and never pay full retail price to look great.

For men, be sure that you wear a white undershirt or tee shirt that covers your armpits with a clean, pressed, long sleeve, white, dress shirt and a conservative neck tie. If you do not know how to tie a *Pratt Knot* or *Windsor Knot*, ask someone for help or use the Internet and view videos on how to tie a neck tie. Be sure that your belt matches your shoes and that you wear socks that cover your ankle and lower part of your leg, and complement your suit color. Be sure that your shoes and fingernails are clean.

For women, wear a dress shirt of any conservative color or pattern. Be sure that your neck line is a standard depth and that you do not show your cleavage…seriously. If you wear a skirt, then be sure that the length is appropriate and touches your knees: do not wear a mini or maxi shirt. You want to be clear that you are marketing your degree and skillset, and not your body. Wear light-weight nylons with a skirt or socks that match your pant suit. Your shoes should be clean, not open-toe, and with a heel no higher than two inches. If you want to be taken seriously as a viable candidate, then do not wear shoes fit for night life and be an easy target for sexual harassment comments.

A note of caution…If you have been successful in obtaining jobs by inappropriately marketing yourself or by flirting or sleeping your way to the bottom, no, that is not a typo, then you may want to consider changing your approach now that you have a college degree. You are looking for a long-term, serious, professional career. Hopefully, you would want to start your new career based on your great skills and education, and gain respect from your peers. (Did I just sound like a mom?)

Frequently, hiring managers do not hire individuals that chose to dress inappropriately for interviews. If the candidate is not able to make an effort to take attention to detail about themselves for the interview, how can this individual be trusted with company resources? Be sure to take attention to detail when dressing for interviews.

Perfume and Cologne

The bath products we use such as body wash, shampoo, conditioner all have scents that help give us a clean scent. Add deodorant, and that is basically all you need to use the day of your interview appointment. Wearing perfume or cologne to the interview is risky for two basic reasons. One, the scent you think is wonderful on you may be the very scent that throws me into anaphylactic shock due to an allergic reaction to your lovely scent. As my eyes tear, as I cough, have difficulty breathing and run to exit the room, I am not thinking I should hire you! Second, these products work on the senses, and humans are not always rationale. For example, the wonderful cologne scent you wear may remind me of the last man that broke my heart and frankly, I hate him…and now I hate you. I cannot hear a word you are saying; all I can do is look at you as I think of the terrible memories about my ex. I do not like him, and now, I do not like you, and…I will not hire you. So, do not run the risk of either situation, and do not wear cologne to your interview.

If you are totally addicted to wearing perfume or cologne and cannot bring yourself to leave your home without using it, or if you fear that your body odor will become obvious as you become warm or nervous, then I recommend that you spray the air and walk through the lingering scent. That may help you and the scent should not be overpowering.

Jewelry

An interview is not to be treated like a fashion show; you are not there to entertain or wow the interviewer with your bling, swag or whatever fancy term your generation may use now. Do not wear a lot of jewelry to an interview. Leave your gems and fancy jewelry at home and be conservative. For men, do not wear earrings – none, seriously. One ring per hand works fine, a wrist watch (as long as you do not stare at it during the interview!) and nothing else. For women, only one set of small or post earrings, only one ring per hand, no bracelets: no ankle bracelets either. If you decide to wear a necklace, be sure to wear something small that complements your business suit.

If you have a nose, lip, tongue or any type of facial piercing, you will want to remove it before your appointment. You may also want to research the company to find out if they have a policy on such items. Some employers require that all customer-facing employees not have any type of facial piercings. If you are not flexible in your stand on facial piercing, you will want to know about their policy before interviewing or accepting the job.

Ink

Most corporations have a policy on tattoos. If your body is a colorful work of art, be sure to do your research on the corporation in attempts to find out their policy regarding tattoos. Some employers require that all tattoos must be covered during work shifts, and some only when dealing directly with customers. Play it safe, for your interview, cover your tattoos with high collars, long sleeves and pants. Everyone has an opinion and freedom about body ink; however, more importantly, employers have the option and freedom to hire people that they believe will follow company policies.

Make-up

If you do not regularly wear facial make-up or if you are not proficient at applying it, then do not start wearing it on the day of your interview. It would not be good if you accidently put too much on your face or accidently poke yourself in the eye with eye-liner or mascara and show up to your appointment looking less than your best. If you are not confident about wearing make-up or about how to apply it, then get some help and practice applying it days before your interview or simply do not wear it.

Also, there is a difference between the make-up you would wear during the day to look professional and then there is make-up that you would wear for an evening event; so, be sure that you do not confuse the two. Do not go to the interview looking as if you were on your way to a nightclub or just came from one!

The color of your fingernail polish may match or complement your outfit. Be wise in choosing a color that will not distract from your marketing pitch during the interview. Keep the length of your nails within reason, not too long, and avoid patterns or designs on the tips of your nails to help keep the focus on you and not your accessories.

CHAPTER EIGHT

Interview Questions

You wrote a great cover letter, your résumé made a good impression, and you receive a phone call to schedule a job interview. Wow – exciting! Then you realize that you need to figure out how to answer the plethora of questions the hiring manager may fire at you during the interview. Suddenly, an overwhelming feeling of uncertainty hits you in the gut. Well, you are not alone. Most candidates feel stressed and nervous thinking about what they will be asked and how will they reply.

Types of Questions

For most interviews, two types of questions are usually asked during an interview, informational and behavioral. The informational questions are just what the name describes; the interviewer is seeking information from or about the candidate. Such questions may include:

- Tell me a bit about you.
- What three words best describe you?
- What is your key strength?
- What is your weakness?
- What challenges did you face while in school?
- What did you like about your degree program?
- What do you know about our company?
- What drew you to apply to this position?

Behavioral questions attempt to provide insightful information about the candidate's behavioral style and pattern. Past behavior may predict future behavior, and most of the questions used during the interview may be behavioral based. Such questions are not really questions; they are statements that require an example and may include:

- Tell me about a time you had conflict.
- Describe a time when things did not go well for you.
- Tell me about a time when you had to admit to a mistake.
- Describe a time when you were asked to compromise your ethics.
- Tell me about a time when you were treated unprofessionally.
- Describe a time when working in a team went well.
- Tell me about a time when working in a team did not go well for you.

Individuals interviewing for health care or medical positions may also need to reply to clinical assessment questions. Engineering candidates may need to reply to math or technical questions. This may be part of the initial interview and may be done verbally or as a written test. In technical interviews, programmers may be given a situation and be asked to write programming code to showcase their skillset and understanding of the process. Some organizations will have a candidate write a letter or email in response to a customer question or compliant.

Behavioral-Based Interviews

Many hiring managers, including myself, prefer to use behavioral based interview questions rather than informational questions. Not only will they ask you an insightful question, they will ask additional probing questions based on their first question. I call this tearing down or leveling down to get to the heart of the situation. Think of an artichoke. You must tear away at each layer of outer peel before you can get to the heart of the vegetable. So with behavioral based interviews, they will be used to peel away at the layers of you and your behavior. Let me give you an example of a question I like to use:

Tell me about a time you had conflict with another person. Walk me through the scenario.

a. When did you first realize there was a problem?
b. What was the result of the action you took?
c. How did you feel when you approached them?
d. How do you think the other person felt when you approached them?
e. Did you learn anything from this situation or experience?
f. Would you do anything differently next time you are faced with a similar situation?

The first question, tell me about the conflict, allows you the opportunity to provide a brief reply; the six, subsequent, probe questions were used to go to the next level of your behavior. Best tip I can provide you about these types of questions, do not lie or attempt to bluff your way through these questions! You need to be truthful and provide sound details about the steps you took, the results, your feelings, and the learning outcomes. This is one of the main reasons that hiring managers love to use these questions! They help see the candidate in a realistic way; so be sure to use good eye contact, positive body language and a positive tone even when speaking about a negative situation.

The SAR Method

Prepare before the interview so that you are comfortable with your answers to the anticipated questions. Do not attempt to memorize what you will say; however, review it and be confident with your replies. Try or practice the Situation, Action, Result method or SAR method. This is a great way to address the question, capsulize the details without going off on a tangent, and stay on course with addressing the question. Responding well to interview questions requires the skill of storytelling. I call it storytelling with a purpose.

Discuss the situation, talk about the action steps you took, and tell them what the result or outcome based on your action steps. When the question is tell me what you consider your strength to be, do not simply reply listening. Provide them an example of how you have used your strength of listening to achieve a benefit or an accomplishment.

> *Responding well to interview questions requires the skill of storytelling. I call it storytelling with a purpose.*

An SAR Example

One of my strengths is listening. *Situation*: My friend, Tim came to me with an issue he was having with another student, Peter, who was on his project team. He told me Peter was not pulling his share of the work on the project and had not attended the last project team meeting. *Action*: I carefully listened for the details of what was going on with the project and the team members. When my friend was done talking, I recommended that he not assume anything and to privately approach the other student. I thought it would be helpful for Tim to ask Peter to meet with him and ask him a few questions about how things were going and the project. *Result*: He did, and later he shared with me that Peter had been recently diagnosed with a serious illness. So, imagine if Tim had jumped all over Peter! They decided to work together and the entire project team came together to complete the project in time for their presentation and they received an excellent grade.

The SAR method is a good to use for several questions and even when you are asked a question you did not anticipate. Let's face it, there are thousands of interview questions! Having and using the structure for a balanced reply may help keep you confident, and compose yourself as you compile your response. Stay with the brief details, talk about the steps or action you took and the result you achieved.

Prepare and practice aloud; practice in front of the mirror to see what the hiring manager will see and hear. This will give you an opportunity to see your facial expressions, your mannerisms, your body language, and posture. Yes, it sounds be tad crazy to stand in front of the mirror and talk to yourself; however, I do this and it works. I do public speaking; I practice in front of the mirror to help me prepare. Every professional athlete and musician practices and thoroughly prepares – why not you? Also, if I were not willing to do this, I would not recommend this to my clients and to you!

Evidence-Based Interviews

The goal of a good interview - using the SAR method and practicing your responses is to be considered the best candidate for the position. You must be prepared to confidently walk into the interview and provide the best evidence: you are the best candidate fit for the organization and for the position. If I had an interview tomorrow, I would be prepared with my research and my questions. I would have invested time in properly preparing responses for their questions, and I would have the evidence to support my case that I am best person for the job. I would have solid examples prepared for the behavioral and informational questions with evidence to support that I am aware of what I do well, my strengths, and the key results I have achieved in my career.

Interviews are not to be taken lightly. This is not something that I could just wing my way through (I have broken a few wings trying!). I would want to be fully prepared; no less than an athlete for a competitive sport or a musician for a recital.

Resource

The author Martin Yate's wonderful resourceful, *Knock 'em Dead* reviews over 200 tough interview questions. The book is widely available through the Internet, libraries, as well as book stores across the country. The book is usually updated annually and has helped countless job seekers. Consult this helpful guide and resource as you prepare for the interview questions, different types of interviews, and interview tests.

The 180 Approach

One of the most difficult interview questions for a new grad may be the combination question *Briefly tell me about yourself and why did you decide to apply to this position.* Most people do not know where to start, what to say, and feel inadequate to talk about themselves. They may wonder, does the hiring manager want to know about me, my school, and my goals? Do not assume that the interviewer only wants to know something personal about you, and do not assume that the interviewer only wants to know something professional about you.

As a hiring manager, I want to know a bit about the person, the individual, as well as about their professional situation, be it work experience or school. You can combine a bit of each in your response. Tell a bit about you, the person, and then why you are in this interview. Relate something interesting and then bring it back around to the interview – 180 degrees: this is what I call the *180 Approach*.

If I were being interviewed for a project managers' position, I might reply by saying something like – *I enjoy living in Arizona, I do not mind the heat. I love to swim and hike, and I enjoy the hot summers. I have over 20 years of successful project management experience in pharmaceuticals, retail, and education, and I am very excited to be here today at XYZ Company to speak to you about this great opportunity. I was drawn to apply to your organization based on the positive information and feedback I received from several of your employees.* I briefly told you about me without mentioning anything extremely personal or private about myself, and then I brought the conversation right back to the interview.

Technical Interviews

Developers or programmers may be given a scenario, a problem to solve, and then asked to write code for the process. If you are invited to this type of interview, here are some things you should know. These interviews may not contain any getting to know you questions, such as tell me about yourself. You may interview anywhere from two to five different times and the interviews may last up to 45 minutes each. These interviews are strictly to test and challenge your critical thinking and programming language skills. Since these types of interviews are grueling, you may be asked to dress comfortably; business casual attire works well, unless the employer let you know it is appropriate to wear your favorite jeans and shirt!

Upon hearing the scenario you may be asked to step to a white board or a computer and write the code sequence to solve the problem. Feel free to talk aloud to yourself to ensure that you are correctly processing your critical thinking skills as you write the code. Be sure to code in your strongest language, Java, C#, C++, Python, Objective-C, PHP, Ruby, or SQL to be confident as you create the solution. If it appears you are not on the right track, the interviewer may ask you questions or give you hints to redirect you back to the correct solution, be sure to be open to their questions and their feedback. This is not the time to be or appear defensive. Be sure to test the code you wrote on the white board or the computer to ensure you have the correct answer.

The key skills you want to showcase in these types of interviews are language syntax, core libraries, idioms, reasonable design, and analytical. In order to keep your skills strong during your job search, be sure to join local or national competitions. You may also consider donating your time to a local organization and volunteer to help them as you continue to keep your skills sharp.

Once the technical interviews are over, the employer may take you to lunch or dinner and at that time may ask you questions about yourself and your interests. Since the employer has already put you to the test, the lunch or dinner conversations may have nothing to do with the interview or the decision to hire you. However, be polite, grateful, and go easy on your caffeine intake before and after the interview!

Interesting Approach

Several major technical organizations as well as mainstream corporations receive millions of résumés per year. They have a challenge in selecting candidates to interview for the many competitive positions. They have adopted a unique approach in asking interview questions. Rather than ask the standard informational or behavioral questions, they ask candidates riddles, puzzles, and unique questions that challenge the candidate's critical thinking skills. One of my favorite questions: *How many piano tuners are in the state of Arizona?*

Interestingly, many of the puzzles or riddles do not have a right or wrong answer! However, the question is given to see how the candidate uses their critical thinking skills, how quickly the candidate can think under pressure, and respond to the situation - even if the situation is seemingly impossible or a ridiculous one, such as the piano tuner question. By the way, my reply would be - *I hope 88 in case I have a question with one particular key!* If you not understand my response, I recommend you find a piano.

If you would like to see examples of some of the outrageous, real interview questions used among some major corporations, visit *Glassdoor.com* and see if you have what it takes to quickly compose an answer to some of the odd situational riddles, puzzles or unique questions. Good luck!

Inappropriate Questions

Occasionally, an interviewer may ask an inappropriate or illegal question. If the interviewers have not been properly trained in the interview process, they may ask an illegal question, unaware that it was wrong. Possibly the interviewer, may ask an illegal question in hopes that the candidate may simply reply to the question and reveal private information without hesitation. Either way, it is wrong. Certain topics are off limits and should never be included in the interview process. Questions regarding age, alcohol or drug use, arrest record or convictions, religious background or ability to work weekends or religious holidays, disabilities, marital status, whether you have children, your height or weight, gender, sexual preference, race, accent, citizenship, your social media login and passwords - all have no bearing on your ability of fulfilling the duties listed in the job description. Some of these questions, such as arrests or convictions, may be legally asked within the job application; however, they should never be addressed in the interview.

When you are asked an illegal question, simply ask how the question relates to the job or the job description. If the interviewer continues to press you for an answer, then politely say that you are aware the question is illegal, and that you feel uncomfortable answering the question. One word of caution, at this point the interview may be over, which may not be a bad thing. You may be told that they may call you for follow-up or you may simply be thanked for your time as you are being shown the door.

You have the choice and prerogative to contact the company Human Resources Manager to alert them of the situation, or you may contact your local *Equal Employment Opportunity Commission, EEOC,* office to discuss the situation. Whatever you do, do not just simply avoid the issue. The *EEOC* provides guidelines to employers and best practices to avoid inappropriate questions and discrimination of interview candidates.

Questions to Ask

As you research the company information before the interview meeting, review articles about company, navigate their website, and review the job description. Generate a list of questions to ask during the interview. Be sure the questions are relative to your interview and the prospective jobs. Be sure to include the list in your portfolio; be prepared to ask the questions either during the conversation exchange or at the end, which is usually when you are asked if you have questions. The list may be handwritten or typed, and be sure to place them in front of you as you ask the questions. This way, even if all your questions are addressed during the conversation, the interviewer has the impression that you made the effort.

However, do yourself a favor and never ever tell them that you do not have any questions! I do not comprehend how or why a candidate would ever show up to an interview without questions. How could anyone consider starting a career with an organization when they do not know about the department, their challenges, their needs, their structure, their culture, the dress code, shifts or hours, and the management style of their potential manager? Ask reasonable questions that the hiring manager will not have any issue discussing with you. Be certain to ask when they anticipate making a decision on the position or ask what the next step is in the process. Have a clear understanding of what is to happen next before you leave the interview.

Test

Some candidates, such as electronics majors, may be required to take a written test before meeting with the hiring manager. Healthcare candidates may be required to do a medical calculation test or to verbally describe medical conditions and drug treatments before replying to traditional interview questions. Candidates interviewing for sales positions or teaching positions may be asked to conduct a presentation on a particular topic. Make sure you inquire if your interview will require a verbal or written test. If a written math test is required, take a pencil, paper and a calculator with you to the interview. If a presentation is required, find out how many people will participate so you bring sufficient handouts. Be sure to verify if a white board is available and bring your markers and an eraser. If you require a projector to use with your computer, or ask if one will be available for you before you arrive for your appointment. If they provide the computer, you can bring a flash drive. You will want to be proactive and well prepared for your presentation.

Many companies' request candidates take a personality assessment to ensure the individual will be a good fit for the position before extending a job offer to the candidate. Some of the questions on the test have a right and wrong answer; some of the questions do not and simply test critical thinking skills. I recall two questions on a test I used many years ago that I administered to sales associate candidates. They were to reply yes or no to each question. The first question, *Is there a difference between smoking a cigarette and smoking marijuana?* I always had a hardy laugh when I would see candidates respond no to this question. Really, no? One was legal and one was not! At that time, the use of marijuana was illegal and the term medical marijuana was an oxymoron and no states had addressed issues on the topic. The second question, *Is there a difference between stealing $5.00 or $50.00 from the cash register?* When candidates would reply no – it made my job easy in deciding on which candidates I wanted to hire!

Smile for the Camera

You received a phone call to schedule an interview, and you are very excited about meeting with the hiring manager. You arrive for your appointment expecting to meet and greet the hiring manager. To your surprise, you are ushered to a room with a computer with a camera. You are asked to sit at the computer and hit the enter button to start your interview. You hear a voice ask you a question, and you proceed to answer the question;

you continue to hit the enter button and proceed to the last question. Once you complete the taping of your interview, someone thanks you for your time and away you go.

Some organizations videotape every candidate interview. The recruiters review each interview session and recommend only the best candidates to the hiring managers based on their findings. The hiring manager will invite only those candidates for a face-to-face interview. This method is helpful because it saves the recruiter and the hiring manager a lot of time and they meet only with qualified candidates.

Two of my clients were invited to do a videotape interview with a company that receives hundreds of applications for open positions. To best prepare them for this type of interview, I videotaped them during their interview with me. They were able to objectively assess the interview, and we discussed the things they did well, and of course, the areas they needed to improve their skills. This helped them see what the camera would capture as well as be confident and prepared for the actual video interview. They did very well and were offered an invitation to meet with the hiring managers and they received the job offers that they hoped to receive. They were happy that they took the extra step of fully preparing this way.

The Internet also allows a candidate to meet with a hiring manager across the country or world, without ever leaving home. This method also allows the employer to save time and money during the recruitment process. If the hiring manager will conduct the interview using a messaging system, again, fully prepare before your appointment. Practice interview questions in front of the mirror or ask a friend to do a practice interview over the Internet with you so that you can see yourself – for yourself! Be confident in what the hiring manager will see for your real interview. Be sure to dress professionally, in a gray or navy blue suit for this interview. Have your portfolio and all your documents available as if you were in the same room as the hiring manager.

Do not make the mistake a recent college grad made during a messaging interview: he wore a white dress shirt, a neck tie, and a suit jacket as he sat at his desk in front of his computer. His hair was combed and he looked neat and professional. When the interview was over, he stood up before he shut off the computer camera. He was in his boxer shorts, and the hiring manager saw more of him than she ever had expected to see during an interview! She did not hire him because he did not seem to be as detailed as the job required. Dress professionally for the Internet interview and be sure to wear your complete outfit. Also, be sure to turn off the camera and all microphones before standing or making comments about the interviewer or the meeting!

CHAPTER NINE

Is Media Really Social?

Today, we have so many social media options - from text messaging, the Internet, and the plethora of websites, to job boards and professional networking sites. I recall my feeling of awe in the early 2000's as I held my slim, shiny, mobile phone and connected to the Internet for the very first time. As I sent and received my first text message, and years later as I downloaded applications to my phone, I was amazed and wondered how these features, these tools would change my life. Little did I know that these tools would revolutionize the globe!

The Internet provides us with countless ways to broadcast and promote our lives. For some people, this has been wonderful and for others it has been the extreme opposite. Some individuals leave a dirty, digital footprint and leave nothing to the imagination of anyone viewing their material, including recruiters and hiring managers. Sadly, their behavior and the instant publication of their lives, has robbed many of potential opportunities. The opportunity to obtain their dream job quickly becomes a nightmare as they try to rationalize their behavior and online presence.

> *Nothing is private on the Internet.*

Digital Dirt

In the last several years, we, society, have been obsessed with the ability to instantly publish the activity of our lives. For some, this has been a great thing; for others, this has been a disaster. As I used to tell my college students, we, this society did not invent stupidity: that happened long ago in a garden far, far, away, in a distant time. However, this society has no issue or forethought about instantly publishing their stupidity over the Internet and mobile applications. This has been a sad and devastating disaster for the countless millions that have either lost some great opportunities for potential jobs or have lost their jobs due to their inappropriate behavior they themselves made available for anyone to view online. Do not make the sad assumption that your site is safe because it is set to private. Nothing is private on the Internet. There are ways to find valuable information on job candidates. So, if you have posted your stupidity on the Internet, attempt to remove it, and clean up your digital dirt and your life before you start your job search.

A high number of recruiters and hiring managers use the Internet to find and research potential candidates. It is imperative that your social media presence be positive and presents you as the ideal candidate, even with your personal and private activities. In some states, there are laws regarding how employers are to treat the personal use of social media by job candidates; however, employers want to hire people that are socially conscientious and law abiding citizens. Also, it is damaging to a potential job seeker when they brag about breaking the law such as with their use of illegal drugs. There may be laws that ask that we disregard what is seen; however, how can information like this not be used in making a sound and wise hiring choice? If you are clearly breaking the law, can you be trusted to abide by company policies and carefully handle company resources? Probably not, and this overt sharing of stupidity is very counter-intuitive. You, your parents, someone, invested a lot of money for your education. I would hope you would want to showcase that your critical thinking skills and sound judgment extend far beyond the classroom walls.

LOL

One of my biggest concerns for current job seekers is that many have lost their ability to communicate effectively. So many high school and college-age students use a short-cut method to speak that saves time and key strokes on their electronic devices. I get it; however, this method of communicating is not the proper method to use to market oneself, write a research paper, a memo, a business letter, a business proposal or an email. When you create a letter for your potential employer it must be well written with proper punctuation and be error free. Otherwise, the employer will *lol* as they chose the next candidate and not you!

I recall speaking with Nathan, he that told me that he thought taking general education courses was a complete waste of his time. He thought that he should only be required to take classes that relate to his major. He was a culinary major and was interested only in cooking and creating beautiful culinary presentations. He shared several of his recipes with me and I was amazed and saddened when I read his instructions. He did not take general or Basic English in college and his recipes were living proof. He wanted to publish his recipes or perhaps open a small bakery. Too bad he did not realize the value of correct spelling and command of the English language, which by the way, was his first and only language. Why would anyone want to purchase a book that was difficult to read with confusing instructions – often due to grammatical errors or purchase bake goods spelled incorrectly on a menu?

Personal Branding

Companies brand products every day, and they do a great job of advertising their products. With a colorful label, a consistent bottle or can color, a logo symbol, a hood ornament, a silly jingle, we can easily recognize a product before we see the name of the item. Advertisers spend a lot of marketing dollars in hopes that their product recognition will mean something to you, the consumer, as you spend your money at the retail register.

As a job seeker you need to consider and think of yourself like a product: what or how are you marketing yourself? You are an individual with skills, experience, and an education - nice; however, you also have a presence and an online presence. Are you branding yourself so that employers would be proud to have you among their staff and as a company asset? You may need to reconsider the branding message you send out about yourself on a daily basis either in person or online. You invested a lot of time and money in your education; advertise it in a positive way to get the job offers you want and need!

If your personal brand, the way you act or behave has not been positive, it is not too late to rebrand. Remove all negative information you have posted on the Internet, including photographs that show you in less than your best life style or show your lack of effective critical thinking skills. Keep only the photographs, comments, and individuals from your contacts that will present you as a responsible, trustworthy, professional job seeker.

CHAPTER TEN

The Interview Process

Interviewing is a process. It is important to have a strategic plan and prepare yourself for the process. The process comprises three phases: before, during, and after. Great candidates will need to attend to many details to ensure they are the best candidate. Here are a few for you to consider. Keep in mind, the before list contains items that you need to attend to days before the interview; some of the items on the list are for the day of your appointment.

Before the Interview

- Shower, shave, brush your teeth; attend to all other basic hygiene routines
- Get a haircut: Do this with sufficient time to feel comfortable with the new look
- Update your voice-mail message to sound professional
- Avoid offensive ring-back tones or inappropriate voice-mail greetings
- Do not wear any cologne or perfume to the interview
- Eat a light meal before you head to your appointment – without garlic or onions
- Call ahead to ask about the location, the cross streets, directions, and parking or use a search engine to obtain information
- May consider a test run and see what traffic is like and know where you will park
- Get your outfit ready; wear clean, well-fitting, professional attire
- Prepare your portfolio and ensure you have sufficient copies of your résumé
- Practice interview questions with a friend or in front of the mirror
- Research the company; review the job description
- Prepare your list of questions
- Visit your social media sites and remove any negative content

During the Interview

- Arrive on time; this really means arrive early
- You may arrive early to the appointment, however, let them know you arrived within minutes of your scheduled appointment time
- Find a rest room close by so you can take one last look at yourself in the mirror
- Turn off your cell phone - yes, seriously
- Politely introduce yourself to the person at the front desk and make a good impression
- Stand, have confident posture and body language
- Give a dry, firm handshake, and smile
- Wait to be asked to be seated in the meeting room
- Offer your résumé to everyone in the meeting and place a copy in front of you
- You may have a business card clipped to résumé or offer a card to them
- Give positive eye contact; do not stare, remember to smile
- Be clear on your skillset and what you have to offer the company
- Be prepared to discuss your research; reply to their questions and ask questions
- Use the SAR method to reply to their questions and support your answers
- Confirm the date when they plan to make a decision on the candidate
- Shake hands with the interviewers and thank them for their time

After the Interview

- Send a hand-written thank you note within 24 hours of the interview
- Follow-up with them on the date they confirmed to you in the interview
- Continue to apply to jobs and network until you receive a job offer
- Keep track of where you applied and the follow-up dates in a job search journal

It Matters How You Shake It

A dry, firm, not bone crushing, handshake will indicate that you are honest, serious about the job interview, and prepared. Hiring managers may take 30-90 seconds to determine if they want to hire a candidate. You have a small window of opportunity to create a professional impression, and a firm handshake will help you create that impression.

If you become nervous and tend to have wet, clammy hands, you have another reason to arrive early to the interview. Take a few minutes to stop in the restroom, run warm water on your hands and completely dry them. Taking a clean, cotton handkerchief with you to your appointment will also help. Be sure that your hands are dry before you shake hands with the hiring manager. If you suffer from extreme perspiration, you may want to consider using a light-weight, clear antiperspirant or speak to your doctor about prescribing a product to help your hands stay dry. Test the product on your hands days before the interview to ensure it works and does not cause any additional issues. You want to leave your interviewers with a positive impression, not a film or white paste on their hands!

> *If you keep track of every job application you submit, you should eliminate the risk of accidently applying for the same job twice.*

The Job Search Journal

Be sure to keep track of every job that you have applied to as well as when to follow-up with the recruiter or hiring manager. You may do this manually on a sheet of paper or you may create an electronic document. Here are some things to track during your job search:

1. Position Title
2. Company
3. Date Applied
4. Did you submit a cover letter and to whom was it addressed
5. Did you do a follow-up call to ensure they received your résumé
6. Date the recruiter called to schedule the interview
7. Interview date
8. Date sent thank you card
9. Follow-up call on date they provided during interview: not sooner

If you keep track of every job application you submit, you should eliminate the risk of accidently applying for the same job twice. As you see from the list above, finding a good job takes time and proactive steps on your part. The job search journal is a handy tool to help you keep everything in order in one place.

Be sure that you follow-up with the hiring manager within the time frames they provided you and not sooner. You do not want to bother the hiring manager or become their best stalker! That is one sure way to get your name removed from the short list of potential, hirable candidates.

The Best of You

Be sure that you are at your best or at the top of your game as you set out to your interviews. In summary, eat a light meal so that your stomach does not start talking during your meeting. Do not eat a large, heavy meal and fall into a food coma and fall asleep during the meeting. Be upbeat, positive and engaging so the person interviewing you does not fall asleep either! Be polite, professional, smile; give a firm (dry, not sweaty, not bone-crushing) handshake, dress conservatively and professionally. Give positive eye contact, have good posture; support your answers with solid examples, and ask questions. Do everything in your power to be the best candidate in order to receive job offers. Concern yourself with the things that you can control and take the adequate time to prepare to be the best candidate you can be for every interview.

CHAPTER ELEVEN

Networking

Over the years and for time to come, one thing has been and will be consistent with a job search strategy: who do you know? Now, please understand, this question is not intended to diminish your great feat and accomplishment of graduating from college. I applaud you – I am happy you chose to obtain a degree; however, your degree alone may not open the right doors of opportunity for you.

Networking, How?

Many college students and recent graduates are faced with the dilemma of not knowing what is it to network, and who it involves since I do not know a lot of people? I define it as the core group of people that you know from every relationship that you have. Here is how *Dictionary.com* defines networking:

Part of Speech: *verb*

Definition: to socialize for professional or personal gain

Synonyms: associate, circulate, hobnob, make contacts, meet and greet, mingle, rub elbows, schmooze

It does not matter how many people you know in order to effectively network; what matters is how you use your network. Include everyone that you know in your network as you seek for a job. I hope you have family, friends, neighbors, class mates, and roommates – good, include them in your network. You have no idea the people each of these individuals may know, and one of them may know the person that may hire you. In an earlier chapter, I talked about branding yourself in a positive way, and here is the main reason to do it.

Your family, friends, neighbors, class mates, roommates will be happy to recommend you to recruiters and hiring managers if you have done a great job of branding yourself as a hirable individual.

> *It does not matter how many people you know in order to effectively network; it matters how you use your network.*

Whom to Include In Your Network?

Shout it from the mountaintops! Tell everyone you meet that you are a college graduate seeking employment. Do you shop at the same grocery store weekly? Good, tell them. Do you belong to a gym or health club? Good, tell them. Do you go to the dentist? Good, tell the receptionist, the hygienist and the dentist. Do you attend church or synagogue? No? Hmmm - well that is another topic for another book! If you attend church or synagogue, tell them. (If not, you can still pray!) Does your campus have a career services department? Yes, talk to them! They are usually a valuable resource and have many contacts and job leads. Everyone you meet should know that you graduated from college, your degree or program, and that you are looking for a job! This is not the time for you to be shy. I tell my clients, *network like the rent is due tomorrow because for some of you, it is, and so are your student loans.*

Here is a list of people and organizations to include in your network.

- Family
- People from church, synagogue, associations
- Friends
- Neighbors
- Co-workers from current or past part-time or full-time jobs
- Former or current supervisors
- People you meet where you shop regularly: stores, barber shop, salons, coffee shops, dentist office, health club, and so forth
- Individuals you met during internship, externship, clinical or medical rotations, and practicums

- Career Services Department
- Faculty and professors
- Peers and classmates
- Recruiters, head-hunters: job search agencies, temp agencies
- Individuals from alumni associations, honor society, student clubs, sports, rotary club, city chamber organizations, and customers

Now What?

So, now that you have your list in your head or better yet on paper, now what? Well, first step is talk to all of these individuals and let them know that you graduated from college, let them know your major, and career interests, and that you are looking for a job. This is another handy way to use your one-page résumé or your business card! Second step, ask them if they know anyone in your field or if they can recommend anyone that you could contact. Your goal is to find out who they know, connect with them to help you with your job search, and get your résumé in the hands of the decision makers or hiring managers. If you decide to contact a job search firm, or better known as a head hunter, be sure to never pay a fee. Do not ever pay a recruiter to help you find a job. A solid organization will collect a fee from the employer they assist. Third step, go online and visit professional social sites such as *LinkedIn.com* and *XING.com*, and set up a professional-looking profile of yourself and connect with everyone you know. Once you connect with them, you can see their connections. Your goal is to find the decision-makers at the organizations where you are seeking employment and, never, never, never, under estimate the power of one connection! When using these sites, be sure to post a (conservative) picture of yourself, include your skills, education, and experience you want to market.

Profile

Create an account with a professional networking site; upload a current and nice head shot picture of yourself. Briefly describe yourself with a few words, not necessarily a job title. Create a summary of your skillset and experience. You may include internship, externship, and practicum information. Highlight your job history, create a detailed skills section, and join groups that interest you. Once your profile is complete, start adding contacts, such as peers in your program you trust, co-workers, and your new networking contacts.

Research the companies that use professional social networking sites and you may be pleasantly surprised to find that someone you know is connected to the hiring manager of the company that has your dream job. Research the job postings and job descriptions to gain an understanding of the types of candidates they seek. Again, you may well discover the company that has your dream job.

Four Letter Dirty Word

There is a dirty word in networking, and the word is work! It is not enough for you to have this long list of people that you know and simply do nothing with it. If you are not working your list, your contacts, then you are not benefiting from your network relationships. Let's think back to the definition of network: to socialize, to associate, circulate, hobnob, make contacts, meet and greet, mingle, rub elbows, schmooze. This means that you actually need to talk to people, spend time with them, and use your network to its best advantage. Stay current with people and let them know your plans. I find that most people are usually very willing to help each other and are excited to help others connect. Keep in mind, it's inevitable and a promise – you will also be in a position one day to help someone else do the same!

> *The power of one connection is incredible. Do not under estimate how one person in your circle of family, friends or neighbors can help you.*

Networking Success

Does this really work? Of course it does! I have used my network of family, friends and former co-workers many times during my career to find a job. I have helped many people connect with key decision makers for positions they have accepted; it works. I want to share some amazing stories of how individuals have effectively used their network to find a job. Yes, I did change their names to protect their privacy.

David was preparing to start his job search. He decided he needed a haircut and headed to the salon. During his conversation with the hair stylist, he mentioned he needed a haircut to be ready for job interviews. She asked him what type of job he was looking for, and she let him know that she had a client in the same industry. After the haircut, she called the gentlemen and she connected the two of them. David received a job offer after meeting with this new networking connection!

Nancy is a hair stylist at a salon. One of her customers, Amanda was in the salon for a haircut. Amanda asked Nancy how her husband was doing in school. Nancy shared that her husband, Curt, recently passed the state board exam and is a nurse, and that he was looking for a job. Amanda said she thought that the hospital where she worked was having a large hiring event the following week and would call Nancy later that day with the details. A few hours later, Amanda called Nancy and gave her all the details. That evening Curt applied and received an invitation to the event and he was offered a position that very day.

Diane met several people during her clinical practicum rotation. She was very upbeat and positive and she was polite, helpful, and professional with everyone she met at the hospital. She made a great impression on everyone she met; she was granted an interview with the hiring manager of the unit and offered a job before she graduated from her program or had even completed an online job application! Oh, and by the way, at the time the company was under a hiring freeze that was lifted prior to Diane's start date.

While attending college, Dan worked at a bank and was very helpful to every customer. Ms. Taylor was a regular business client and Dan had the opportunity to assist her with her banking needs. Ms. Taylor owned and operated an accounting firm. She appreciated Dan's helpful manner and attention to detail, and she frequently requested that he assist her. During one conversation, Ms. Taylor let Dan know that she thought he would be an asset to her company and offered him a job. She also let him know that she would be willing to cover part of his college tuition. Dan was thrilled and amazed that he was able to receive such an amazing job offer by merely by providing excellent customer service to his client.

I received a phone call from James. He let me know that someone he knew told him about me and recommended he contact me. I asked how I could help. He heard that I had several contacts with a local company that interested him. I listened as he told me that he wanted a project manager's position with the organization. I told him we would start with his résumé and he sent me a copy to review. I updated his résumé to better showcase his skills and accomplishments. I asked him who else he had included in his network, and he confessed that he did not have many people in his circle. I recommended that he start talking to everyone he knew including his neighbors. A few days later, James called me to let me know that he started talking to his neighbor and was amazed to learn that his neighbor worked for the same major company where he wanted a job! That neighbor introduced James to several other neighbors that worked for the same company. The neighbor across the street introduced him to someone at their church and through that contact, James received an interview for his dream job and was offered the position.

Karen worked a part-time job while she attended college. She wanted to stay with the company full time after she completed her degree. Karen was granted an interview for a full-time job and received the job offer. As soon as she was hired, she contacted a few of her close college friends and was able to get their résumés to the hiring manager. The hiring manager interviewed Karen's friends and extended job offers to them.

Cindy's friend and neighbor, Sandy, was expecting a baby and invited Cindy to her baby shower. Cindy had recently graduated from college and had applied to a position with a major hospital. As the women at the baby shower were being silly and enjoying good banter and laughter, Cindy started a conversation with one of the women. The woman, Martha, turned out to be the hiring manager for the position at the organization where Cindy applied. Suddenly, Cindy took a moment and mentally re-ran each word that had come out of her mouth and had hoped she had not behaved in a negative way during the party! A few weeks later, Cindy had the opportunity to interview with Martha for the position and she received a wonderful job offer. Later, Cindy shared with me that she learned the value behaving professionally everywhere she went and how small the world truly is.

Jared worked at a major electronics retailer with Ed, a friend from college. Jared received a job offer for a network support technician position from an organization that attended a career fair that was held at his college campus. He enjoyed his new job and the culture at the organization; he told his friend Ed to apply for a position. Jared asked Ed to let him know as soon as he applied to the support tech position. The following day, Ed sent Jared a text message to let him know that he submitted the job application. That morning, Jared let his supervisor know that his friend Ed applied for a tech support position. At that very moment, the supervisor was reviewing résumés and told Jared to have Ed stop in to chat with him. Jared immediately called Ed and gave him directions to the location. That afternoon, Jared introduced Ed to the supervisor and Ed was hired on the spot.

Personal Networking

A former co-worker of mine, mentioned that she was an adjunct instructor for a local university and she let me know how much she enjoyed it. A few months later, she told me two positions were posted at the university that may interest me and I applied for both positions. I was granted an interview for one position within career services and was offered the position and I accepted the job. Two months into the new job, I was asked to co-teach a class and within a month, I took over the class and taught for three years.

Many years ago, while in college, I worked in a nursing home as a nurse assistant and I had briefly considered a nursing career. Sadly, I was physically attacked by a patient and this dangerous encounter helped me decide to continue with a business degree. I had no interest in staying with the nursing assistant job, and I told my friends and family that I was searching for a new job. A few weeks later, I had the opportunity to interview for a full-time position where I could use my accounting skills, and I happily accepted the job offer. The job I interviewed for was never posted and I was able to interview for it because of one of my personal contacts.

When I lived and worked in the Chicago area, I met a business and technical writer that created training modules for the organization where I worked. I had the opportunity to participate in several of his presentations and he and I connected on other projects. As I was thinking about leaving my job, he inspired me to move forward with my writing projects, and he invited me to collaborate with him on a writing project for a pharmaceutical company. He inspired me to be an independent writer, for which I am very grateful. Although, that was a few decades ago, I am grateful for his friendship and I will never forget the opportunity to work with him on my first free-lance writing job. When I decided to publish my last book, I reached out to him for help. I needed an editor that I could trust and give me insightful feedback, so I reached out to Steve. He was also willing to help me with this project and I appreciate his sharp editorial pencil and guidance.

Steven Schultz, Ph.D., is the president of *Writing at Work*. He started his business in 1985 and focuses on training business and industry professionals to produce effective documentation. He writes, he edits, he teaches, and creates amazing training materials. When you are in need of creating detailed procedures, he is the man for the job! I am proud to call him friend, and he is the person I trust to provide me with excellent feedback. Networking is important to him since he depends on his networking abilities and his reputation as he continues to grow his business.

Unlike Steve, I operate a small, writing business. My own networking is tailored to my small business model and personal lifestyle. I enjoy creating training manuals and I am a professional résumé writer. Wait - before, you search for my company on the Internet, I will tell you, I only work on projects by referrals and I do not have a website. That may surprise you; however, I network with individuals that are interested in my services, I create documents for them and then they refer me to other clients. When I receive an email or phone call from a prospective client, one of my first questions is *how did you get my contact information*? I only work by referral, so networking is very important to me. The main reason I do this is, is the *birds of a feather, flock together* concept. If I have a great client, I will assume they will promote my services to the great people they know. This helps me and keeps my life less dramatic and, of course, keeps me safe when I have to meet with a client, which I do in very public places.

The power of one connection is incredible. Do not under estimate how one person in your circle of family, friends or neighbors can help you. Be sure to keep your network current and be kind to others as you use your network for good. Also, remember to be willing to help someone else along the way! You may be able to land your dream job and, in turn, someone you know may want to speak to you about working for your organization and so forth. Treat people the way you would want to be treated; play well in the playground of life!

CHAPTER TWELVE

Where Are The Jobs?

In the previous chapter, I discussed the value of using your network to find a job. One great reason to network is to find the jobs that never make it to the job boards, like the accounting position I mentioned in the previous chapter. Some companies cannot afford or want to spend hundreds of dollars to post positions on electronic job boards. These employers depend on employee referrals and recommendations to fill positions. This saves them time, money, and will hopefully bring quality candidates to the organization. This is another major reason why personal branding is so important. If I have a qualified and quality employee working with me, I start with the assumption that they will only refer someone like themselves for an open position. This is the *birds of a feather, flock together* example that you may have heard from your parents or grandparents. I will assume that if you are a good employee, you will only refer another good employees.

The Hidden Job Market

These positions are usually not posted to Internet job boards and are marketed and recruited for by current employees - word of mouth, job placement agencies, career services departments, and via a confidential posting by direct hire firms. When you are well connected to employees of a certain company, you will have access to the non-published jobs and have an opportunity to market yourself for positions through your connections. I routinely receive email notifications asking if I know of anyone that could fill positions that never hit the Internet job boards. I forward the job leads to individuals I know may be interested. Recommended key contacts is an effective way for the employer to find qualified candidates quickly.

I once received a phone call from a recruiter who needed to fill a sales manager position. The job was not posted anywhere but with her office. The company was attempting to keep it quiet that it was bringing in new managers for three of its locations. I gave her the names of a few individuals that I thought might be interested. Within a week or so, she called me back and asked me if I would be interested in the position. She let me know that she researched me and my sales experience and thought I would be perfect for the job. I considered the offer to interview. I did my own research on the organization and I accepted her invitation to meet with the vice president of sales.

Job Boards

Today, there are countless electronic job boards on the Internet available to you. Use job boards that will search various sites for open positions and bring you all of the results in one search. These sites are called aggregators because they bring total results from various sources into one search. A few examples of such sites are *Indeed.com, SimplyHired.com, Jobwall.net, CareerBuilder.com, Monster.com, CraigsList.com, Glassdoor.com, and Dice.com.* You are able to do an advanced search for jobs by company, key words, job title, and city and state. You are able to set up email alerts and have the job postings sent to your email as soon as they are available.

You may also use *Linkedin.com* to find jobs by the company name, job title, or key words. You may follow a company and receive email alerts as the job postings become available. Several employers use *Facebook.com* to post internships and opportunities for new grads. Use the *like* option to follow their activity. Use *Google Alerts* or *SocialMention.com* and receive email updates on the companies you follow. Check the job listings in *Twitter* by using their *twitjobsearch.com.*

Taking It to the Streets

Many job seekers are taking the old-fashioned approach to their job search and taking it to the streets. They are proactive in their marketing and not waiting to be found on résumé sites. You can be proactive and ask to meet with the recruiter or hiring manager and put a face to a name before or after you submit an online application. I know many individuals where this has worked nicely for them. They were proactive, dressed professionally, they were granted a brief meeting, and the hiring managers accepted their résumés.

In one case, Jill, a new grad that took my recommendation, was hired on the spot when she asked to meet with the recruiter. The recruiter introduced her to two managers that had open positions within their departments. They gave her the choice of the department to work and she started her new job the following week! Another new grad, Troy, who took my recommendation - with much fear and trepidation, he walked into the organization and asked for the recruiter who briefly met with him. She was impressed with his résumé, suit, and extreme proactive job search approach. Within a week of his courageous visit, she reached out to him and asked him to apply online for a position she posted for him. In an email, she provided a link to the job posting for him apply. Based on her wonderful recommendation, he was granted a formal interview with the hiring manager. The recruiter told the hiring manager she was very impressed with his proactive behavior and appreciated that he wore a suit the first day they met. He received the job offer at an organization where he did not know anyone prior to his visit.

One thing to keep in mind as you take your job search strategy to the streets - this may not work with some government organizations. Remember, I mentioned that they do not think outside the box; they may not welcome your proactive approach to walk into their office and ask to speak with an individual. Their knee-jerk response to you may be go away and apply online. You may be bold and ask for the business card of the recruiter, which in some cases will not be given to you; however, smile, say thank you and walk away. With these types of organizations, it is best to use any internal contacts you may have to help you with your efforts.

Informational Meetings

If you are not certain if a particular job or career path is for you, reach out to individuals within those industries or positions. For example, if I were interested in a particular position and wanted to know what it takes to get there, I would want to interview a person who currently holds the job. Offer to buy them a cup of coffee and ask them questions. If I were interested in knowing about a manager position within a large hotel in my area, I would contact the manager and offer to buy them a cup of coffee and interview them. They would probably be flattered at my request and grant me a one half hour appointment for an informational interview and talk about themselves!

At one point in my career, I considered taking more course work in education to obtain another degree and pursue a career path to become a university campus president. I scheduled an appointment to meet with John; he was the president of a local university. I asked him about his career and the career path he took. I listened as he talked about teaching at the university level for several years, how he became the dean of a program, dealt with curriculum issues and the hiring and firing of faculty, and he shared the details of what his current position involved. After carefully listening, I asked him one question. How much student interaction did he have? He replied, little to none. I knew one thing – I no longer had an interest to become a campus president! His life was filled with local and national meetings and numerous reports and had such limited exposure to students. I was so happy and fortunate that he allowed me the brief meeting and gave me the details of his position. This truly helped me to consider other options on my career list.

Digital Footprint

Other venues to market your skills are sites such as *YouTube.com*, *MySpace.com* or *Goggle+*. Create a believable and honest video of yourself to market your skills, your work samples, your art, and degree. Use sites that allow you to showcase your skills or artwork or photography in one place using content curation tools such as *Pinterest.com* or *Lostly.com*. Upload your photography to *Flickr.com* and provide a link in your résumé to your work. Create a website to showcase your skills and work samples and provide the link in your résumé. There are several options on the Internet to use to create a free website or network with web developers from your college or university to get low cost help with your site. Use social media in a positive way to help you market your skills, education, and work samples.

> *As always, it is vital that everything you post and upload presents you in a positive, professional manner.*

Digital Résumé

The wonderful thing about using a personal website, content curation, or a business social network site is that hiring managers can find you and obtain more information about you than with just one document. Many recruiters use the Internet to search for viable candidates. They use the key word search to find candidates, so for many of us our digital footprint is our résumé. It is wonderful to know that it is so convenient today to apply to a position right from a professional networking site. At the click of a button, I can apply to a job and use my social media profile as my application. This means I must always have my profile current and I do not need an additional document to apply to jobs. I recommend that you update your profile and take advantage of this feature when applying to jobs. You may still need the paper résumé for the interview; however, using media makes the application process extremely convenient.

Another great feature of social media networking is that at a glance recruiters can review your skillset, work samples, experience, and feel confident about contacting you based on your online presence. As always, it is vital that everything you post and upload presents you in a positive, professional manner. You have wonderful, creative, and unique skills that employers need, so ensure that you convince them to contact you to discuss your abilities.

Internet Resources

I did some research to find organizations that offer helpful information to college graduates, including job boards. At the time of printing this guide, all of these sites were active; as the Internet changes constantly you will want to regularly update this resource list as needed. These sites address the needs and questions of recent college graduates. Feel free to visit any or all of them for some good information and helpful resources.

For general information:

Career One Stop	www.careeronestop.org
College Grad	www.collegegrad.com
O*NET Online	www.online.onetcenter.org
The Job Hunter's Bible	www.jobhuntersbible.com
The Riley Guide	www.rileyguide.com

When researching company information:

Career Journal	www.careerjournal.com
Corporate Information	www.corporateinformation.com
Hoovers	www.hoovers.com
Manta	www.manta.com
U. S. Securities and Exchange Commission	www.sec.gov/edgarhp.htm
Vault	www.vault.com

For salary information:

Glassdoor	www.glassdoor.com
House Moving and Relocation/Salary Calculators	www.homefair.com
Indeed	www.indeed.com
Job Star Salary Survey	www.jobstar.org/tools/salary
NACE Salary Calculator	www.jobsearchintelligence.com
Payscale	www.payscale.com
Salary	www.salary.com
Salary Expert	www.salaryexpert.com
Wall Street Journal Salary Info	www.careerjournal.com

For information on company or industry trends:

Corp Tech	www.corptech.com
Indeed	www.indeed.com
Job Hunt	www.job-hunt.org
Occupational Outlook Handbook	www.bls.gov/oco
Wet Feet	www.wetfeet.com

For relocation information:

Find Your Spot	www.findyourspot.com
Homebuyer's Fair	www.homefair.com
Money Magazine's Best Places to Live	www.money.cnn.com/magazines/moneymag
Realtor	www.realtor.com
Sperling's Best Places	www.bestplaces.net

For information on military or government jobs:

Clearance Jobs	www.clearancejobs.com
CPOL: Civilian Personnel Online	www.cpol.army.mil
Hire Vets First	www.hirevetsfirst.gov
Transition Assistance Online	www.taonline.com
USA Jobs	www.usajobs.gov
Vet Jobs	www.vetjobs.com

Job Search Sites:

CareerBuilder	www.careerbuilder.com
College Grad	www.collegegrad.com
Education Linked	www.educationlinked.com
Find Jobs	www.findjobsz.com
Hot Jobs	www.hotjobs.com
Indeed	www.indeed.com
Job Central	www.jobcentral.com
Jobs 2 Careers	www.jobs-to-careers.com
Quintessential Careers	www.quintcareers.com
Retail Jobs	www.allretailjobs.com
Simply Hired	www.simplyhired.com
Snag a Job	www.snagajob.com
State Jobs	www.statejobs.com
Thing-a-ma-job	www.thingamajob.com
US Jobs	http://us.jobs

For information on job search documents:

Career Lab	www.careerlab.com/letters
Job Star	www.jobstar.org/tools/resume/index.htm
Portfolios	www.amby.com/kimeldorf/portfolio

Social networking for jobs:

85 Broads	www.85broads.com
Be Known	http://beknown.monster.com
Brazen Careerist	www.brazencareerist.com
Facebook	www.facebook.com
GadBall	www.gadball.com
Jibe	www.jibe.com
Jobster	www.jobster.com
LinkedIn	www.linkedin.com
My Workster	http://myworkster.com
Ning	www.ning.com
Twitter	www.tweetmyjobs.com

CHAPTER THIRTEEN

Show Me The Money!

He or she who mentions money first always loses, I say. During the first interview, it is never a good idea for the candidate to mention money. It is the candidate's job to convince the hiring manager that they are the best person for the position based on their skills, education, and experience. When the candidate mentions money first, this may be perceived as being greedy and the individual's motives for wanting the job may be questioned. Let the hiring manager discuss salary first and be prepared to confidently discuss the topic.

You Want How Much?

It would not be wise to walk into an interview and have your first or even last question be about money. It would also not be wise to ask for a salary that does not match the position, location or business size. Let's say, I had an interview in Phoenix, Arizona, for a CAD Programmer position with a small organization. I assume that since I just graduated from college (and have student loans to repay), I should be making some big bucks. I let the hiring manager, Ms. Wright, know that I am interested in the job we are discussing, and oh, by the way, I am looking to make $55, 000 per year. She lets me know that the current salary she is offering is $30,000 per year since she owns a five-person operation. Then she proceeds to tell me that, oh, by the way, the top salary in the valley for this type of position is $37,000 per year, as she shows me the door.

The opposite could also hurt and work against me. Using the CAD Programmer position as an example, let's say, during the interview, I let the hiring manager know that I am interested in the position. I would be happy to take the job for $28,000 per year and she offers me the job at that salary. Unbeknown, she was prepared to offer me $30,000; I was overzealous in asking about money, and now she is saving money by offering me less.

Do Your Research!

To avoid either mishap, do your homework and research the current salary for the position for the city in which you are searching for a job. The salary for an accountant in New York will be much different for the same job in North Dakota. Also, consider the salary difference a big box manufacturer will pay versus a mom and pop shop around the corner.

Visit sites such as *Salary.com, Indeed.com* or *Glassdoor.com* to review the most current salary ranges for the positions in the cities that interest you. If you are considering relocating or debating staying in your current city, then run a salary comparison for both cities to get a realistic range to help in your decision.

Salary Range

When it is the appropriate time to discuss money, it is usually safe to talk about a salary range rather than a fixed number. If the hiring manager for the CAD Programmer position wants to know what salary I expect, it is safe for me to say something such as: *Based on my research, I see the current salary range for this position is between $32,000 and $37,000 per year.* I can then ask the question: *This the position that we are discussing in that range?* At that time, the hiring manager can tell me yes or no or simply tell me how much she is offering.

Always be prepared to discuss the salary range when the hiring manager is ready to discuss this topic. The hiring manager may discuss salary in the first or second or third interview. It may be discussed when you receive the job offer – there is no set pattern; however, whenever the subject is brought to the table, always wait for the hiring manager to bring up the topic first and always be prepared for the discussion with your research!

> *Without my research on the current salary range, I would not have the confidence to address the topic of money or even dare ask if the salary is negotiable.*

More Please!

I have been asked several times if it is acceptable for a candidate to ask for more money than they are offered. My reply is, you may ask; however, you must do your research, consider the company size and earnings, the location, and know the acceptable salary figure you want, based on your research. It is acceptable to ask; however, be prepared for the employer's response either way.

When the employer says no – then they mean no. They made the offer and await your response to accept the job or turn it down. If they say yes, they may place the burden back on the candidate and simply ask them what salary they want and determine if it is doable based on their budget.

Let's go back to the CAD Programmer position. At the end of the interview, the hiring manager, Ms. Wright, tells me she is impressed with my work samples and thought I had interviewed well; she offers me the job at $28,000 per year. I simply ask, Ms. Wright if the salary is negotiable and she says no – that is her offer, take it or leave it. However, if she tells me, yes – she may simply ask me what salary I am I looking for at this time. I would let her know that based on my research, I was hoping to obtain a salary between $30,000 -$32,000 per year. She may tell me that she will consider it and get back to me within a day or two. If she calls me the following day and offers me $31,000, I would let her know that I appreciate the new salary offer, and accept the position. She matched my salary request within the salary information I shared with her. I would accept the offer and be happy she was able to offer me more money than she originally intended to offer me. I would be done with the salary negotiation.

Without my research on the current salary range, I would not have the confidence to address the topic of money or even dare ask if the salary is negotiable. As a new college graduate with little to no experience, I do not recommend attempting to negotiate a salary with an employer since other than your education, you may not bring much more to the organization. Salary negotiations are usually for experienced candidates; however, if you attempt such a conversation, be prepared with your current research and do not be too disappointed if they say no - and be pleasantly surprised if they say yes!

Benefits

Do not ask right away about benefits during your interviews; again you do not want to look greedy. Wait for the employer to discuss them with you. Most organizations list their employee benefits on their website, so you will be able to view the information. During the time of the job offer, the Human Resources department discloses all the necessary information to the candidate regarding the start date, salary, benefits, sign-on bonuses, along with additional information a new hire would need. This is a great time to ask questions, and clarify anything that you are not sure about, and allow them to explain the information. Keep track of the open enrollment dates for medical insurance and any other important dates.

Sign On the Dotted Line

Most employers provide a written job offer to their new hires. Be certain to thoroughly read the hiring agreement before you sign it. Ensure that whatever was verbally promised to you during the job offer conversation is listed in the job offer documents. If something is missing or incorrect, do not sign the document. Be sure to contact the Human Resources department or the hiring manager immediately so that they can make the corrections and send you an updated contract to sign.

Be sure you sign and return the documents within the agreed time frame that you discussed or the date that is written in the contract. When you sign the contract, you agree with the terms and agree to keep your part of the agreement. If you suddenly decide not to accept the position, then be sure to get back to them right away and do not sign the contract.

CHAPTER FOURTEEN

Background Checks

In their job offers, employers use safe language such as *offer is contingent on candidate passing drug test and the background check.* Employers want to hire candidates that will be honest with company resources, budgets, company assets, and time. One method that is used to evaluate an individual is a criminal background check.

Not So Good

If you have an arrest record, be sure that you complete the job application by replying honestly to such questions. If the question asked, have you ever been arrested, then be sure to reply, yes. If the question is have you been arrested in the last five years, and your incident occurred six years ago or longer, then you will be safe in replying, no. Be truthful and never, never, lie on a job application.

You will want to write a brief statement on the job application stating that you will be happy to discuss the details of your record within a separate private meeting. This way, you are not disclosing the details of your situation on the application and you are offering to talk in private regarding your past if necessary. This would be a separate conversation from the interview, assuming you not disclose or discuss such information during the job interview.

Before you face this situation, I recommend reading *Job Interview Tips For People With Not-So-Hot Backgrounds,* by Caryl and Ron Krannich. This is a good resource for anyone with negative backgrounds needing solid advice. It provides information on your legal rights within the process – which many of us do not know.

Never More

Be sure to reply honestly to the job applications questions; however, do not disclose or discuss your negative background within the first interview. You may need to meet or speak separately with someone in the Human Resources department to provide brief details. Prepare a brief statement in advance for the possible discussion with the Human Resources Manager about your negative background, past behavior, and police record. Be sure to include things such this past, is no longer part of your life, what you learned from your choices and mistakes, and the commitment to yourself and others regarding your current choices. Employers may address these topics with you; however, they are not to discriminate against you because of your background. Since we do not live in a perfect world, and if after this discussion, they decide to pull the job offer, you may need to have further conversation with them or the EEOC.

Keep in mind, though, if you have a police record for petty robberies, the local bank may not want to hire you to be a bank teller or a personal banker. If you have a police record for drug use and possession of narcotics, you may not want to apply for a sales position with a pharmaceutical company. With these types of positions, the employers will want or are required to hire individuals that have a clean background record with no police issues since the job description is clear on its qualifications. With these types of situations, you will not have the support or guidance from the EEOC since the employers' requirements are clear within the job posting.

Probation Period

Most companies have a policy on a 30-, 60- or 90-day probationary period for all new hires. This means that the employer has the option to release an employee within that time if they are not working out as they hoped or planned. If the employer is willing to hire you in spite of your negative background or police record, they may ask you to agree to a shorter or longer probationary period to ensure that you will be a stellar employee as you committed to in the interview and when you signed the offer letter. Many organizations are willing to give new employees the benefit of the doubt or a second chance; it is up to you to be willing to show them that they did not err by offering you the position.

If the conditional probationary period is offered to you, try not to take this personally. Please understand the employer is offering you an opportunity and is merely taking precautionary measures to protect their reputation and company assets. You may want to seriously consider taking their offer. Use the probationary period to showcase your degree, your critical thinking and other skills, and your work ethic. Make sound and wise choices for yourself and your new employer. This type of probationary period is usually not tied into or connected with employee benefits, so be sure that the offer letter is clear on this point.

> *If you have anything on the Internet that may be considered offensive, inappropriate, and illegal, now's the time to clean up your online presence.*

Oh, That Was So Wrong

As stated in an earlier chapter, your online presence may be viewed by your new potential employer. So, when they see that photograph of you, half-naked, drunk, and holding illegal drug paraphernalia, do not be too surprised when you are not the candidate of their choice. As mentioned earlier, some states have laws to protect candidates regardless of what employers see about the potential new hire; however, it is very difficult for me and anyone else to not place some level of opinion, judgment or critical thought about seeing someone half-naked and holding illegal drug paraphernalia! So, regardless of the state you live in and the laws that may impact your improper postings, clean up your act.

Present yourself so that you can confidently represent and market your education, degree, skills, and get a job! This is the time to start making a return on the considerable amount of time and money you or your family invested in your education – think seriously about your behavior in order to get and keep a job.

The Internet may be used to find out about you and your social life, your associations, and may be used along with the background check. Right or wrong – that may be for the legal system and the courts to decide; however, for now, know that your name and your online activities are viewed and used as consideration by employers. Take a look right now. Search your name on the Internet and see what everyone else sees about you. You may also want to run a search to see how many people have lost their jobs due to inappropriate behavior, inappropriate language, negative criticism of co-workers or bosses, drug use, crimes, and other questionable behavior they decided to post (themselves!) on social sites. Remember, employers invest a lot of money in finding and hiring candidates that will be law-abiding citizens, keep their company policies, and represent them in a positive manner. It is an expense for a company to recruit, hire, and train a new employee; they want to ensure they invested spending their recruitment dollars wisely.

Where They Will Look

In addition to spending money on a background check, the employer may also check the local county court records and sites such as *Pipl.com, YouTube.com, Mylife.com, Myspace. com,* and *Facebook.com.* Not long ago, a great website called *DigitalDirt.org* brought together in one place court records, social media, photographs, and any Internet mention of a person's name. This website was a handy resource to quickly obtain a global perspective on any individual. At this time, the website is inactive, but others are replacing it that make searching for information very convenient, frightening, but convenient.

If you have anything on the Internet that may be considered offensive, (regardless of your opinion) inappropriate, and illegal, now's the time to clean up your online presence. Understand, as you may already know, once it is on the Internet, it never really goes away; so start showcasing your good deeds and present a positive and legal side of you. It makes sense to choose to continue that type of behavior, not only to receive a job offer, but to maintain employed regardless of your opinion on these issues. Keep in mind, you want a job, you need a job, and your school loans will not repay themselves! Let's face it, you are an adult now and I would hope that you would want to start living a responsible, adult life. I would hope you would want to earn the respect of your peers, do a great job in your position, and enjoy the financial rewards of living a responsible life. (Yes, I did just sound like a mom, didn't I?)

CHAPTER FIFTEEN

Accepting or Rejecting a Job Offer

You conducted yourself in a professional manner during every interview in hopes of obtaining a job offer. Your phone rings, not once, but twice with job offers. You are so very excited and now must decide which job to accept – this is a nice problem! You will say yes to one job and no to another; however, you want to be polite, professional, and not damage any relationships while turning down a job offer.

Thanks, Yes!

You want a job, you need a job, and you would be happy with any job; however, you also hope that you receive a phone offer from a second company with your dream job. Always thank the hiring manager or human resources manager for the call and the job offer. If you need a day or two to consider the offer, it is acceptable to ask for a reasonable time frame, a day or so, to get back to them. Call back within the agreed time frame of two days and let them know that you are interested in the job and ask how soon you will have the offer packet. Take a few days to consider and review the details of each job offer. Be sure to review the offer packet to verify all the details that you discussed and agreed on are included before you sign the document. If something is missing or stated differently than you discussed, contact them immediately so they may send you a new corrected offer letter. Do not assume the corrections or changes will be made at a later time; obtain the revised copy to sign before you start the new job.

> *When you turn down a job, use words such as at this time: At this time, I will not be able to accept this position.*

No Thanks!

When you decide not accept a position, call the employer within one to two days and let them know. Be polite, professional, and thank them for everything they have done thus far. Let them know that at this time, you will not accept their offer. Keep in mind, though, at some point you may need to re-connect with them. If the job you originally accepted, your dream job, becomes a nightmare, you may consider re-contacting this employer, so proceed with caution.

When you turn down a job, use words such as at this time: *At this time, I will not be able to accept this position.* You may let them know verbally over the telephone and you may also write a letter that they will keep in your file. This way, when you decide to re-contact them within a few weeks or months, hopefully they will remember you as a professional, polite candidate. You may be granted another round of interviews. During that time, they will want to confirm that you will accept their offer if they decide to extend one to you. You may have to go through the entire hiring process one more time before they do. You may be fortunate if a similar position opens or their original candidate did not work out, and they may simply offer you the job. Either way, give them an answer within a reasonable time and be certain to sign and return the offer letter - also within a reasonable time.

CHAPTER SIXTEEN

Developing Your Career

You did everything right and landed the job of your dreams, nice. You head to work your first few weeks and suddenly you start to feel a bit less confident. You wonder if your degree fully prepared you for your job. You begin to question your skills and abilities and you feel quite stressed. Well, welcome to your new career!

As a new college graduate, you may feel a tad unprepared for your new career and the enormous responsibilities; this is normal. One thing that will help with this frustration is to ask questions and seek direction from your new supervisor or manager to ensure that you are doing a great job.

The rest of this chapter, discusses some basic things to consider for managing your career in an effective manner. Some of the information may be familiar to you since they are considered common sense; however, I find that sense, sadly is not all together common.

> *I wish I could tell you that your new boss will be supportive, a great inspirational leader, a problem solver, and will provide guidance to you every step of the way; however, we do not live in perfect world.*

Communication

The one skill that you possess that your new manager will appreciate is effective communication. Be sure to ask questions – this is part of being an effective communicator.

This will help you as you attempt to be clear, dependable, and will aid in eliminating miscommunication and conflict. This will be very helpful when you discover that your new manager may only be a manager by title. Managers do not always lead by example, and they may actually take credit for all your work. I wish I could tell you that your new boss will be supportive, a great inspirational leader, a problem solver, and will provide guidance to you every step of the way; however, we do not live in perfect world. I wish I could tell you that your new manager will be a great communicator and excellent at resolving conflict; however, sadly, some of you may work for an awful person. However, this does not release you from being an effective communicator and strive to do the best job you can in being clear, open, honest, and positive.

Please and Thank You!

Polite – Sometimes in the workplace people forget the basic principle of being polite to each other. At times, co-workers or managers can be aggressive with requests and tend to forget that everyone deserves to work in a professional and respectful environment. One basic way to be polite with co-workers is to use polite language. When you need assistance, say please along with your request. When a co-worker has provided information or assistance to you, say thank you. This literally takes seconds to do and will aid you in creating and maintaining a polite and respectful environment. You will find that people will tend to want to assist you, and you will help build a good relationship with your co-workers.

Own It!

You arrive at work one day – it is a beautiful day. The sun is shining and you are humming your favorite tune as you stroll to your desk. As you approach your desk, you find your manager, not smiling as she stands with her arms crossed. As you stop humming and slow your pace, you realize, she is not happy. She asks you to step into her office and she closes the door. As you take a deep breath, she lets you know that she is aware of a costly error you made the previous day, an error that has either impacted the department or the organization, and not in a good way.

You realize that yes, you made the error and now you have a choice to make. You take the high road - admit to the error, apologize, and offer to fix the issue. Or, you deny it – you blame others, and behave defensively. Take the high road: admit to your mistake, own it, apologize, and move forward. Things to keep in mind, you are human and you are allowed to make mistakes and face failures; however, I hope and trust you have the courage to face up to your mistakes. Also, understand, even the most careful, detailed individual is capable of making a mistake, so you cannot be too critical about yourself.

Admit to your mistakes, attempt to remedy the problems, and maintain a positive relationship with your manager. I believe that I learn something new about myself each time I make a mistake, and I definitely learn about myself when I fail. With failure, I have two choices; I can persevere or I can give up. Failure will drive me to either respond in a methodical way, or drive me to react negatively. However, I have learned to stop, breathe, evaluate my situation, and move forward positively from the teachable moment. Muster up the courage to own your mistakes and use the experiences as a teachable moments in your life.

Training and Education

Be sure to keep current on business trends, associations or publications that affect your industry. Subscribe to and read trade journals or publications that relate to your career, business type, products and services. Be aware of changes to regulations, laws, equipment or processes that affect the way you do business. When training, conferences or continuing education is offered or made available to you, make this a priority. Be a life-long learner. You will want to continue to develop your skills as you continue to grow in your career. Remember, it is your career, so do the things that you need to develop and enhance it. Most companies have a policy on tuition reimbursement, so find out the steps you need to take to use your benefits.

As you continue to add credentials to your name, be sure that you keep a level head about yourself and your accomplishments. Never use your credentials as a weapon towards anyone nor hide behind them because you are more that the credentials. Do not think of yourself more highly than others merely because you decided to continue your education. You, the person are more than these credentials and your credentials do not define you. I once had a co-worker that insisted that everyone call him doctor – he was not a medical doctor but he did have an advanced degree in science. He projected a sense of superiority around the office and many in the office did not care for him or his attitude. Don't let this happen to you.

Play Well On the Play Ground

While in school, you may have worked on a team in order to accomplish a project and learned the value of working well with those individuals to meet a specific goal. Well, now that you have a job, you may be called upon regularly to work with a team of people (that you may or may not like) to accomplish a task, complete a project or report. Perhaps you are asked or told or better yet, *volun-told* to be on a diverse committee to meet a goal. In any case, you will want to make an attempt to work well with everyone you meet. You may or may not like people, any people; however, for the value of keeping your job and accomplishing the task, you will need to do your very best to get along with everyone. Working effectively in a team may require you to put your differences aside, respect your fellow team members, and compromise for the value of the task at hand. It will require that you take a sense of ownership of your responsibilities and be a great team player.

Working well in a team will also mean that you put aside your feelings and learn to respect your fellow peers so you can civilly accomplish the task at hand. You will want your peers to respect you and you will want to learn the value of respecting your co-workers, regardless of your personal opinion of them. This may not be a simple or easy task, because sometimes, it is not. However, for the sake of getting along and for your career path, you will want to get along with everyone and respect your co-workers and managers.

To gain valuable insights about working well within a team, read *The 17 Essential Qualities Of A Team Player*, by John C. Maxwell. This is an awesome account on how to be an effective team player and be the person every team wants on their team.

While working as a lead project manager, I recall being asked by the company president to serve on several of his special task force teams. I worked with him for several years and he knew me to be extremely (and brutally) honest and could trust me and my project status reports. I was honored when the president lead one of the team meetings by telling the team that he knew he could depend on me to be honest with my project tracking and status reports. He designated me as the project lead. He knew I would never lie to him regarding the status of a project or actually about anything else. I was very blessed to be the person he wanted on his high level teams.

Generation Why?

Another great reason to play well in the playground relates to the workplace's extremely diverse setting. Not only will you have the opportunity to work with the opposite gender, individuals from various cultures, countries, political and religious backgrounds, you will work with various generations. Today, the workforce is populated with individuals from five separate generations. Possibly, the first time in history that this has occurred. Each generation has its own set of ideals and values. The oldest generation did not grow up with the Internet, and the youngest generation never knew a world without the Internet! Working with such diverse generations may be challenging and fun at times. Enjoy and appreciate the differences. Each generation has its own way of dealing with power, control, conflict, and respect of their fellow employee. There are key similarities within the generations; however, take individuals at face value and avoid stereotypes.

Workplace Generations

Of the tons of information in books, articles, and the Internet about the generations, here is a breakdown of the diverse generations:

1925 – 1942	Silent Generation
1943 – 1960	Baby Boomers
1961 – 1981	Generation X
1982 – 2005	Generation Y or Millennial
2006 – Current	Generation Z

If you work for a traditional company, your organization may be owned or operated by a Silent Generation leader. This individual knows the value of an honest day's work, is hardworking, values respect, control, and most likely, is set in their ways, - not a huge fan of change. They appreciate a personal meeting, a phone call, and a letter in the mail. You may work for or with a Baby Boomer: they value education, being a team player, hard work, and not big fans of conflict. They like personal interaction, a phone call or an email. You may work for or with a Generation X individual who is able to adapt to change, and strive for a work-life balance. They appreciate email or a text message. You and many of your co-workers may be Generation Y: you grew up with and value the Internet, have diverse relationships, and value leisure time. They like a quick email or a text message. For Generation Z, they value the Internet, their profiles, their identity, and many may have been raised in less than traditional homes, may have less structure, less or different morals and values. They like a text message or any instant publication of information.

Talk about your diverse team? Wow, some days you may need a score card just to keep track of you and your co-workers! Each generation has different values, structure, communication style, and priorities. Have fun learning about your co-workers within the different generations, and do your best to effectively communicate with them. Also, if you have the privilege to work with a member of the Silent Generation, spend some quality time with them. They probably have some amazing stories to share with you about their background, their failures, their successes, skills, and life. Take the opportunity to glean helpful tips from this generation before they leave the organization or sadly, die. Baby Boomers possess skills, specialties, and solid experience and accomplishments. You will benefit to learn from this generation; however, you may have a little more time, since most of them may not necessarily retire soon. Besides a desire to continue to contribute to the organization, changes in the economic demands have made it increasingly difficult to retire by 65 years of age.

Manage Change

The old saying still holds: One thing that will be consistent in your environment will be change. Just when you start to feel comfortable on how you are expected to handle situations, the location of your desk or office, the policies, how you get along with your manager, you may be asked to start doing things differently. As you hear yourself scream like a young school child, pull your hair, and kick your trash can, remember it is not about you. Change happens – whether we agree with it, see of the value of it, understand it, or like it; it happens. Change happens in every industry, every company, every department, on a regular basis. You can either continue to kick your trash can, leave the organization, or learn to adapt to the change. There is no value in behaving childish or complaining or making other people miserable with your negative attitude. Ask questions; however, understand that sometimes management will make decisions that impact the overall business, and they do not owe each employee a reason or explanation for the change. So, sometimes, we simply need to get over it, accept it, and positively move forward regardless of the change.

A classic book on change is *Who Moved My Cheese,* by Spencer Johnson, M.D. Dr. Johnson uses a simple, yet profound story to show the value of change, the results it brings, as well as the consequences when we lack the willingness to adapt to change. The lessons in this book are great to use for your personal and professional life.

Heard It on the Whisper

It is Monday morning and as you walk to the office coffee machine, you anticipate a good conversation or hardy banter about the last night's big game. However, as you draw closer you see several co-workers huddled around a quiet discussion. As you draw closer, you hear them say something awful about another co-worker. This is the moment of truth – do you join the discussion, tell them to go directly to the person they are roasting or simply walk away? Office gossip may be a killer – it's best not to join the conversation. We are all entitled to our opinions; however, if you want your co-workers and managers to take you seriously, avoid the office gossip pool at all costs. Keep in mind, your co-workers may be just as quick to be judgmental and cruel about you when you are not in the coffee room!

Also, do not assume that the person that is giving you the latest gossip is your new trusted friend. Let's say, you make this assumption and disclose or share something with this person. Later, you realize that they spread the details of your conversation around the office gossip pool, or they have gone directly to the person that you spoke to them about in private. Neither situation is good or good for you and your career. Stay away from the gossip pool and be discrete with your conversations. Better yet, when you have an issue with someone in your office, go directly to that person and discuss it!

You Have a Spot...

A great way to ruin your career and the respect of all your co-workers is to be a yes-man or yes-woman. Most people unpleasantly call this brown nosing. I will tell you one thing: *grow a back-bone.* Do not be that guy or gal that constantly agrees with bosses just to be on their good side. Do not be the bosses' personal office spy or errand-boy or girl. If the manager has been a manager for more than seven minutes, they will recognize your actions. A smart manager will meet with you in private and ask you to stop your behavior since they will not appreciate your actions. A stupid manager will love the attention, your false loyalty and will find ways to manipulate you. They may also find additional ways to continue to use your services - that is never a good situation. So, do not act foolishly and schmooze the boss. Get some self-respect; wipe your face - get back to work!

Dealing with Conflict

Conflict – the mere word could cause you to be sick to your stomach. Some people would rather avoid conflict than deal with someone else's opinion or attitude. For others, conflict is a sport. Either way, dealing effectively with conflict is a skill. When you are faced with conflict, attempt to calmly discuss the issue with the individual with whom you have the conflict. If you have personal feelings about the other person, such as I do not like you – that is not conflict that is a criticism or a personal opinion. When I come to you to tell you that I do not appreciate you yelling at me in front my peers or clients that is a conflict.

As difficult as it may be, leave anger and feelings out of the equation and talk about the issue at hand. Use I-statements, such as I think, I believe, I sense, to take ownership of your attitude and perspective; avoid blaming. If you make an attempt to work out the issue with others, find they are receptive, and are able to resolve the issue, then that is awesome. However, if you attempt to speak with an individual who is not willing to help resolve the issue, you may want to use the chain of command. Do not fear going to management or the Human Resources department, especially whenever you are confronted with extreme cases such as verbal or physical threats, harassment, illegal behavior or any hostile behavior exhibited by a co-worker or manager. Everyone has the right to work in an environment free of hostility.

If you find that you are a victim of harassment, illegal behavior or a hostile situation, do not fear, you have legal rights and laws that protect you. Take appropriate action: tell the individual to stop the behavior, document details of the situation, and contact your local Human Resources department to alert them of the situation. This department is responsible for discreetly investigating the situation and taking the necessary corrective action. You may experience the unfortunate situation where the worst offender is the senior manager, the president or chief operating officer, or even the manager from the human resources department. You may feel as if you have nowhere safe to turn to with your problem. In extreme situations such as this, you will need the courage to step outside the organization with your problem. You will need to document the details of the incidents and seek legal help.

One of my favorite books, *Your Rights In The Workplace,* by Barbara Kate Repa, J.D. is usually never far from me. I use it to research workplace situations, legislation, court decisions, and stay current with employment laws. When you are faced with serious issues, turn to this resource if or when you find that your organization does not handle it in the upmost respectful or legal manner. The book is updated on a regular basis so be certain you find the current edition. It provides insight on your legal rights, the key steps to take in the process to resolve the problem, as well as resources available to you.

Workplace Violence

Another good reason to try to resolve conflict with co-workers is sadly, you may work with an extremely aggressive and, perhaps, violent individual. You may have to work with someone that is passive-aggressive who is not adequately equipped to deal effectively with problems. You may have to work with individuals who are full of rage and they verbally or physically attack when they sense disagreement, conflict, or criticism. Within a second, they may become combative and may use violence to end a disagreement. Situations like this may not be easy to predict, so proceed with caution when dealing with co-workers. The old saying *you cannot judge a book by its cover* is also true of people. Someone that looks normal or like a balanced individual may not. Watch for clues about the people that you work with and be on guard when dealing with an explosive individual.

On the bright side – according to the US Department of Justice, Bureau of Justice Statistics: *from 2002 to 2009 the rate of nonfatal workplace violence declined by 35%.*

Was That You or Me?

Keep a running list and details of your accomplishments; this is your career, so keep track of it. Do not depend on your memory, because the passing of time and your manager may rob you of your accomplishments. Keep track of the great things you do such as projects, especially those completed early, on time and within budget. Did you increase profits or revenue, did you save the company time or money by implementing a new system? Is there an awesome customer experience you handled or any other major accomplishment you achieved? This list may come in handy when you ask for a merit increase, during your annual review, or as you update your résumé and prepare for your next interview.

That's a Date

To date or not to date a co-worker? This has been a long time question. I do not recommend dating a co-worker for several reasons. Things may start out great, you both like each other, and then the rumors start, this is never good. Then as your relationship progresses, or gets serious, the company policy requires that one of you must change departments, units, or locations. You may still need to work together on projects or tasks and attempt to keep the work relationship separate from the personal relationship. Then, one day, sadly, the relationship dies and dissolves or worse. It lingers like a bad disease and affects your co-workers, and not in a good way, everyone loses. Also, when the dating relationship involves a boss and a subordinate, at some point the boss may be accused of favoritism; that is never a good thing. If the boss decides to promote the subordinate that she is dating, the other employees will not be too pleased with her or her decision, even if she made the best decision for her department. Also, if your boss or manager is dating or married to the manager of the human resources department, where do you safely go to discuss the problem you have with your manager? This makes for an uncomfortable or awkward situation for everyone.

A word of caution if you do date someone from work, keep it discreet. If you meet someone special, then respect the other person by keeping your personal and private life, private. Do not give your co-workers the opportunity to make you the center of the office gossip. Worst yet, if you are a casual dater or player, and have no interest in a real or serious relationship and you are simply only interested in having sex with your co-workers, know that truly few will respect you, at least no one with a functional frontal lobe. If you are you are known solely for sleeping around with everyone - whether you like it or not, your behavior and critical thinking skills, or lack thereof, will be judged. This reputation may be the thing that keeps you from being taken seriously and may ruin your chances for advancement or promotions.

Yes, there are examples and cases of two people who meet at work, date, keep their personal and professional lives separate and live together and even get married. Those exceptions happen. Keep in mind, you worked hard to land your job and for some of you, your dream job. Workplace romances can cloud the waters and add unwelcome drama and pressure of a dating relationship into an already pressure-filled career path; proceed with caution!

Keep It Clean

I would hope that someone, somewhere in your life provided you with good advice about the use of foul language. Few appreciate foul language in a professional business setting or actually anywhere else. Off-color language in a meeting or with co-workers creates an uneasy, distracting, work environment. Since it is considered offensive, this is also a form of harassment. If you have a bad habit of swearing, you may want to consider cleaning up your act before you make the mistake of using foul language with peers, your boss, or clients. Even though you might hear someone nervously laugh, it's not appreciated. You may soon find yourself visiting the human resources office.

Kevin probably wishes he had not used foul language at work, since it cost him his job. Kevin was a customer service representative with a webhosting company. A customer was having issues with creating her website on their site and called with a plethora of questions. She freely admitted that she was not very tech savvy and needed assistance. Kevin explained and re-explained the steps she needed to take to complete the task. The customer was still having issues and Kevin became frustrated and short-tempered. He quickly placed the phone on mute and proceed to say something such as, *"This stupid _____ is so _____ dumb."* To his astonishment, he heard her say, *"You know I can hear you, right?"* Kevin was dumbfounded and quickly apologized; however, she let him know that she would be speaking with his manager. That day Kevin lost a job with an amazing company. When Kevin shared this story with me, I laughed, but not at his behavior – I found humor that for a tech savvy person, he failed to ensure the phone was actually on mute!

Ethics

I know we live in an era where some people think that they can define ethics or integrity based on situations; however, regardless of one's opinion, there is a difference between right, wrong, legal and illegal. I believe that we each need to make a personal, conscientious, daily choice to live ethical lives. Integrity is an important part of a person's character and moral fiber. If you live a life that is led by integrity then you will be able to withstand the temptation when you are asked to compromise your values or ethics. One day, a co-worker or manager may ask you to lie, falsify documents, give false information to a customer or withhold valuable information from upper management or investors. You will need to make a decision to live by your ethical and moral standards and compass, or you will crumble under the pressure and make a bad choice.

When you take the high road and be honest, you communicate your integrity and the fact that you do not compromise your ethics. Be clear that you do not want to be involved with any questionable activities. This may not always be easy since the person that is attempting to control you or pressure you may be the same person that can fire you. Keep in mind, one very wrong decision on your part may be the most costly mistake you ever make. One wrong, illegal decision may end your career. Every day the news is filled with reports of workplace mishaps the ended in prison.

Many years ago, I was asked to compromise my values at the workplace. I took a very vocal position that I would not regardless of the manager's decision. I let him know that I would not lie to protect him or the company under any circumstances. He was not very happy with me, actually, he was very angry with me. Sure, he could have fired me from my job; however, I knew I made the correct decision to stick to my moral standards. Later, he shared with me that he was happy I was firm with my decision and he knew he could trust me with anything! I learned a valuable lesson that stayed with me for a long time. With every boss or manager I ever had, I let them know to never ask me to lie for them. This way, they will also know that I would never lie to them.

One for the Road???

It is never a good idea to get drunk with co-workers. Well, frankly, I do not believe it is ever a good idea to drink alcohol to the point of abuse or becoming inebriated. Having a social drink with co-workers is a fine way to relax and develop camaraderie. I simply do not recommend getting drunk with them. When you chose to drink yourself *three sheets to the wind*, you are in no position to make rational decisions and you run the risk of damage to your personal brand and reputation. You may make the wrong decision to go home with a co-worker or a manager. You wake up not knowing how you got there or even know what happened to you, and wondering where you left your clothes or parked your car. You may need to face and deal with shame, confusion, rejection, and the office gossip pool. Or you may decide to drive home from a company party, get stopped by the police, or worse, cause an accident, land in prison, and be the not-so-proud owner of a new criminal record. Getting drunk is not worth it – so think before you drink. Make a decision and conscious commitment to yourself to not get drunk, especially with co-workers. If you have a problem with alcohol abuse, please get help. Your employer or your medical insurance may provide you with resources to overcome this addiction. Take the first and difficult step in making a tough decision to change your life and be healthy.

Solutions

Most managers probably wish they had a sign on their door that reads, *complaints not welcomed.* Let's face it, most managers are busy dealing with schedules, dead-lines, budgets, employee issues, their own bosses, and are not interested in hearing complaints from their subordinates. One thing to keep in mind, it is never a good idea to park yourself in your manager's office and simply vent about an issue. Whenever you have a problem, an issue, or a concern about how things are done, or not done, bring possible solutions for the problem you want to discuss. Be prepared to show the support you have on how to improve or solve a problem, not simply vent about it. Be proactive and creative and develop a method to resolve the problem. Your manager will be more receptive and willing to give you time to present your solution-driven recommendations. You may be pleasantly surprised to have your new idea, recommendation or method implemented.

Work Life Balance

This is one area that may become a challenge over time. Usually with your first job out of college, you are not bogged down with the pressure and weight of the success of an organization. As you progress in your career, as you move up the corporate ladder, you may find that you work more than 40 hours in a week in order to meet deadlines, project timelines or be successful. You may need to travel more, provide more customer support, track more projects and create more reports - all of which may rob you of quality time with your family or friends. You may face a higher level of stress and your job or manager demands more and more of you. You will be faced with a decision, a tough decision at best. Do you invest all of your efforts for your job or will you know where to draw the line? You may need to discuss this with your manager, and if things do not change, consider moving on to the next stage in your career. I recommend that you do what is best for you and your family and never sacrifice your quality of life, your health or well-being for a job.

Too Much to Handle

When you have trouble coping with workplace issues, I recommend professional help. Your employer may offer you a benefit of a phone number to a help line or other professional services. You may need to speak to a doctor about physical problems, make an appointment. You may need help dealing or coping with a workplace issue, a personal problem or loss and need to meet with a counselor or therapist, do it. Get help for any issue that creates problems for you at work or when work problems that are creating personal problems for you. If pride stands in your way of seeking professional help, get over it. You may be facing an overwhelming situation that you cannot handle or deal with alone, and you need guidance, assistance, or medication to help you function. You may need to take a vacation or personal time to focus on your situation or health. Your mental and physical health are important and too important to ignore.

If you were to break your arm or leg, you would seek medical help and use the aid of a cast, crutches, medication, and take time to focus on getting better. The same goes for your emotional, mental, or physical problems: seek professional help, and focus on getting better. Your health and emotional well-being is very important and you will function and cope better at work and your personal life when you take the appropriate steps to focus on being healthy.

I know this all too well. After my son Jeremy died, I took several weeks off from work. Losing him was sudden and extremely traumatic. I needed time away from my job to get help and effectively deal with my loss. Again, several years later, when my step-son, Joel died, I took time off to deal with the overwhelming, sudden loss and many details I had to deal with on his behalf. Sometimes, life hits us in an unusually difficult way; however, we can take usual and routine ways to get help to deal with the emotions, mental, and physical challenges.

As I mentioned, some of these things may seem or be common sense to you; however, they may not. Be sure to take care of yourself, your behavior, and your reputation as you start and develop your career. Please know that a developing your career must not always involve climbing a corporate ladder, since a rewarding career truly comes from doing what you love. I will admit this took me some time and a few different careers to understand and appreciate this concept. I had the amazing opportunity to expand my borders and create or design the way I wanted my job to be and enjoy it. I understand that you may not have the opportunity to do what you love early in your career. You may need to work a traditional job to learn and gain experience in your field. However, I hope that in time you will have the amazing opportunity to do what you love, what you do best, and create or design your career and be content. Do a good job, deal effectively with others, and most importantly, take care of your own well-being along the journey.

CHAPTER SEVENTEEN

The Holistic Approach

I am a firm believer that the right job is out there for each of us at the right time. One reason I firmly believe this is because I am a person of faith; faith in the Lord Jesus Christ. I believe that God has a plan for me and I need to seek out His plan for my life. I believe that God brings people into our lives at the right time in order to work His perfect will for our lives. We just need to be open to the possibilities and be aware of His working in our lives.

Every time I have needed a job or was considering moving to a different company or considering a career change, the Lord brought new people in my life at the exact moment I needed a connection into an organization. I believe that through prayer and surrendering my life and plans into the Lord's hands, I allow Him to work His way, His plan for my life. For this reason, I include prayer and Bible reading as part of my daily routine. I, in no way am perfect, nor do I strive for it, and I have many weaknesses; however, I believe in a perfect God. My faith in Christ is about the personal relationship I have with Him and not the denominational name on the front door of a church and not a set of rules for my life. I am a non-denominational Christian and I believe it is about the freedom I have in Him to worship Him and the attempt to please Him and honor Him with my life, my life which is a work in progress.

At various times when I needed to find a new job, I included my job search in my daily prayer time. I also asked friends and family to pray specifically for God's lead and direction for my next career move. The Lord has always opened the door of opportunity for me at the right time, and for this I am truly grateful and I know that I am very blessed. I have been purposeful with my prayer requests since I was in high school. I recall needing to find a job the summer of my senior year in high school. I had to quickly save money to relocate to South Carolina for college. In speaking with one of my classmates, she mentioned that she heard about a job not far from our neighborhood. She and I applied and we were both hired. I knew that was a direct answer to prayer. I was able to work to earn enough money to start college. Even then, without knowing it, I was networking, and I had faith that God would answer my prayer. I learned a valuable lesson many years ago about praying for specific things and how God allowed me to connect to the right person at the right time in order to get my first job.

> *I know the plans I have for you declares the Lord, Plans to prosper you and not to harm you, plans to give you hope and a future.*

You may or may not be a person of faith; you may or may not be a person of prayer. You may or may not believe in the supreme power of God or understand or care to know anything about Him. However, as a Christian, as a person of faith, as someone that has witnessed the power of God, I find it a privilege to share my faith with you, along with my holistic approach for my job search. I challenge you to place your desire of finding the right job within God's hands, and allow Him to show you what He can and will do for your life. You have nothing to lose and everything to gain when you receive His blessings for your life.

So pray, mediate, sing, give praise to the God who loves you and truly wants the best for your life. Humble yourself before the Lord Jesus Christ; give Him your heart, your life, and then stand back and see the amazing things He will do for you because He loves you more than you could ever imagine. God's love is amazing and beyond my human comprehension. He gave His Son Jesus; the scripture verse John, Chapter Three, verse 16 (KJV) reads: *For God so loved the world that He gave His only begotten Son.* One of my favorite verses from the Bible is from the Old Testament, in the book of the prophet Jeremiah. The verse is from Chapter 29, verse 11(KJV): *I know the plans I have for you declares the Lord, Plans to prosper you and not to harm you, plans to give you hope and a future.*

Several years ago, when the economy started taking a negative turn, I was laid off from my job. I focused on finding a new job and like most job seekers, I was not offered an interview every time I applied. Another advantage of having faith and practicing my faith with my job search is that my faith helped me to have a thick skin *per se*, as I received rejection letters or rejection email. If I did not have the faith and courage to continue my job search, and if I were completely devastated with every thanks-but-no-thanks response, I would have been doomed. I am not saying that I was not disappointed. Of course I was;

however, I realized or understood that every rejection put me one step closer to where I was supposed to be at that time. After giving myself time to deal with the rejection, my faith encouraged me to keep going and I continued my job quest. I worked my network smarter, and continued the process until I reached my goal. This was not always easy; however, with my faith, God's word, God's direction, my family, close friends and our united prayers, I knew I would have the courage to continue the process. Then one day, my phone rang; my friend and former co-worker let me know about a job opening that she knew of and recommended that I apply. Within a few days, I received an invitation for an interview for a job I accepted. Again, I knew that this was a direct answer to prayer.

Not All about Me

I learned one valuable lesson by having faith in God: my life is not totally about me. I know that may sound crazy, however, I do not control every aspect of my life - although some days I do make this bad assumption. God has given me abilities, skills, and I am blessed; however, I am not totally self-reliant or self-sufficient. I did nothing special to earn the abilities or skills that I possess. I recognize that God has blessed me. I am grateful for the blessings, the gifts He has given me. He has provided me with wonderful opportunities to use my abilities and skills and work with some amazing people and exciting projects. Trusting Him with the details of my life knowing that He has everything under control puts me at ease knowing that I do not have to worry.

So I want to encourage you through your job search process, and may the Lord bless you as you find the job He has for you. I want to share a few more verses from the Bible as I close this chapter. I enjoy reading the King James Version of scripture because I truly love the old English and find this translation accurate. However, you may use *BibleGateway.com* or *Bible.com* to find easier versions to read and comprehend. This section of scripture is from the sixth chapter of the book of Numbers in the Old Testament; verses 24 through 26:

The Lord bless you and keep you; The Lord make His face shine upon you and be gracious to you; The Lord lift up His countenance upon you, And give you peace.

So my prayer for you is that you would believe, trust, and know the Lord and that He would pour out His blessings to you. May the gracious Lord give you peace as you trust Him with your life; He will lead you to the right job, at the right time, and to a fulfilling career.

CHAPTER EIGHTEEN

And - The Beat Goes On

At some point in your career, you may consider the greener grass with another organization. You may be interested in furthering your career, taking on a new challenge, leaving your boss, or simply seeking different opportunities. Whatever the reason for you to start your new job search, the process starts all over again. You will need to take the same steps you did when you obtained your first job. You will be able to find a new job by researching companies, networking with everyone you know, creating or updating your job search documents, and polishing or refining your personal brand.

Regardless of the year on the calendar, the job seeking process will be the same as discussed in the earlier chapters. You may need to update or revise your online brand within the social media resources you use. You will need to research the organizations where you will consider working. You will need to visit their website, read their mission and vision statements to ensure you agree with them and would be able to support them. You will need to network with everyone you know in order to find and connect with the decision makers within the corporation. You will need to revise your résumé and attempt to network to get your résumé in the hands of the decision maker or use your social networking profile to apply for a position. The process remains the same, so be sure to treat your résumé and your social networking profile as a living document, continue to update it with new and relative education, training, certifications, degrees, skills, titles, and accomplishments.

CHAPTER NINETEEN

In Closing

I have a great passion to help people find the right path for their lives and fulfill their dreams. I especially enjoy working with college students because they are the future, have so many questions, and want to learn how to be successful. I find college students eager to want to do things right and are motivated and excited to finish college and begin their new career. It is very exciting and rewarding when they follow my advice and receive the job offer, hopefully of their dreams. I am blessed and honored to have been part of their exciting journey.

As I mentioned in the Introduction of the book, I wanted to pass along some resources and tools to college students, especially my own children. Thinking back to when I graduated from college, it would have been wonderful if someone in my life effectively guided me through the job-seeking process or mentored me. I hope that my own children see me as a mentor and as someone that truly cares about them and their future. As a parent I want to ensure that my own children are better prepared than I was so many years ago when I completed my undergraduate degree.

I am truly honored that you decided to read this guide, and I hope that you found the information helpful. I trust that you will use the information to help you market yourself for your new career, and recommend it to your 100 closest friends! As I mentioned earlier, there are no easy steps in the process. Each step takes forethought, planning, and execution of a strategic plan. You were successful in completing your degree, so I know you will be successful in putting together your plan and properly acting on it.

Remember, to use your personal brand for good and network with everyone you know. Get your job search documents in the hands of the decision makers. Use your online presence in a professional and positive way in order to find your dream job. Focus on marketing your skills, experience, and new degree, and apply to jobs with companies that have a good reason to hire you. Do your research and prepare well for your interviews. Follow up on your job applications and continue applying to jobs until you receive and accept a job offer.

Control the things in this process that you can control. You cannot control when the employer will make a decision to hire you; however, you can show them the evidence on why you are the best candidate and why they need to hire you!

Your Future

Congratulations on your momentous achievement as you graduate from college! If you are one of the many college graduates wondering what they will do with their majors and their lives, please know that the world has so much to offer you and you have so much to offer the world. Your degree is part of your journey and know that your career is part of it. You have the world at your feet, take the first step in making a path for yourself; go invent your life and love it. Do what you love in this life so that you feel fulfilled and content, and know that what you do makes a difference in someone's life. Your first job out of college may be one of many you may have in life. From the time you finish college to the time you retire, you may reinvent yourself and your career several times, so be sure you enjoy the journey. Some of you will have the amazing opportunity to design your careers with innovations, technology, and creativeness, and that is extremely exciting.

So, go forth and get a job! Live your dream. Safe travels on your journey and I wish you the very best as you start your new career. Peace to you.

BIBLIOGRAPHY

85 Broads. (n.d.). *85 Broads*. Retrieved October 18, 2013, from http://www.85broads.com

BeKnown. (n.d.). *BeKnown-Monster*. Retrieved October 17, 2013, from http://beknown.monster.com

Best Places to Live | Compare cost of living, crime, cities, schools and more. Sperling's BestPlaces. (n.d.). *Best Places to Live | Compare cost of living, crime, cities, schools and more. Sperling's BestPlaces*. Retrieved October 16, 2013, from http://www.bestplaces.net

BibleGateway.com: A searchable online Bible in over 100 versions and 50 languages. (n.d.). *BibleGateway.com: A searchable online Bible in over 100 versions and 50 languages.* Retrieved October 15, 2013, from http://www.biblegateway.com

Bolles, D. (n.d.). Job Hunters Bible. *Official Site for the book What Color is Your Parachute.* Retrieved October 16, 2013, from www.jobhuntersbible.com

Brazen Careerist. (n.d.). *Brazen Careerist*. Retrieved October 17, 2013, from www.brazencareerist.com

Build and cultivate your own community - Ning.com. (n.d.). *Build and cultivate your own community - Ning.com.* Retrieved October 18, 2013, from http://www.ning.com

Bureau of Labor Statistics. (n.d.).*Occupational Outlook Handbook.* Retrieved October 16, 2013, from www.bls.gov/ooh/

CareerLab®. (n.d.). *CareerLab®.* Retrieved October 18, 2013, from http://www.careerlab.com

Careers and Career Information. (n.d.).*Your pathway to career success.* Retrieved October 16, 2013, from www.careeronestop.org

Code..., M. (n.d.). Largest source of military transition assistance information and jobs for today's veterans. *Largest source of military transition assistance information and jobs for today's veterans.* Retrieved October 18, 2013, from http://www.taonline.com

College Grad | CollegeGrad.com. (n.d.).*College Grad | CollegeGrad.com.* Retrieved October 18, 2013, from http://www.collegegrad.com

College Grad. (n.d.). *College Grad Career Center.* Retrieved October 16, 2013, from www.collegegrad.com

Corporate Information. (n.d.). *Delivering the Financial World to You.* Retrieved October 16, 2013, from www.corporateinformation.com

CPOL ARMY MIL. (n.d.). *Civilian Personnel OnLine.* Retrieved October 17, 2013, from www.cpol.army.mil www.clearancejobs.com

craigslist > sites. (n.d.). *craigslist > sites.* Retrieved October 16, 2013, from http://www.craigslist.org/about/sites

Dictionary.com - Free Online English Dictionary. (n.d.). *Dictionary.com - Free Online English Dictionary.* Retrieved October 16, 2013, from http://dictionary.com

EBSCOhost Online Research Databases | EBSCO. (n.d.). *EBSCOhost Online Research Databases | EBSCO.* Retrieved October 16, 2013, from http://www.ebscohost.com

EEOC Home Page. (n.d.). *EEOC Home Page.* Retrieved October 16, 2013, from http://eeoc.gov

Facebook. (n.d.). *Connect with friends and the world around you on Facebook.* Retrieved October 16, 2013, from www.facebook.com

Find a Job from thousands of listings with Thingamajob.com. (n.d.). *Find a Job from thousands of listings with Thingamajob.com.* Retrieved October 18, 2013, from http://www.thingamajob.com

Find Jobs. Build a Better Career. Find Your Calling. | Monster.com. (n.d.). *Find Jobs. Build a Better Career. Find Your Calling. | Monster.com.* Retrieved October 18, 2013, from http://www.hotjobs.com

Find Jobs. Build a Better Career. Find Your Calling. | Monster.com. (n.d.). *Find Jobs. Build a Better Career. Find Your Calling. | Monster.com*. Retrieved October 16, 2013, from http://www.monster.com

Find Your Spot | Find Your Spot. (n.d.).*Find Your Spot | Find Your Spot*. Retrieved October 18, 2013, from http://www.findyourspot.com

Find, Share Information related to your location, be found on lostly.com. (n.d.).*Find, Share Information related to your location, be found on lostly.com*. Retrieved October 16, 2013, from http://lostly.com

GadBall. (n.d.). *Account Login | Build a profile, search jobs, career tools for job seekers by GadBall*. Retrieved October 17, 2013, from www.gadball.com/login.aspx

Glassdoor – an inside look at jobs & companies. (n.d.). *Glassdoor – an inside look at jobs & companies*. Retrieved October 16, 2013, from http://glassdoor.com

Google Alerts - Monitor the Web for interesting new content. (n.d.). *Google*. Retrieved October 16, 2013, from http://www.google.com/alerts

Google+. (n.d.). *Sign in and start sharing with Google+*. Retrieved October 16, 2013, from https://plusgoogle.com

Hastings, R. (n.d.). Generational Differences Exist, But Beware Stereotypes. *Generational Differences Exist, But Beware Stereotypes*. Retrieved October 23, 2013 from http://www.shrm.org/hrdisciplines/diversity/articles/pages/generational-differences-stereotypes.aspx

Home | Jibe. (n.d.). *Home | Jibe*. Retrieved October 18, 2013, from http://www.jibe.com

Homefair. (n.d.). *Relocation Calculator*. Retrieved October 17, 2013, from www.homefair.com

Hoovers. (n.d.). *Company Information*. Retrieved October 16, 2013, from www.hoovers.com

Hot jobs for Veterans; Resume Search, free job posting, free resume hosting. (n.d.). *Hot jobs for Veterans; Resume Search, free job posting, free resume hosting*. Retrieved October 18, 2013, from http://www.hireveteransfirst.com

How to Job Search, Explore Careers and Get Educated | Riley Guide. (n.d.). *How to Job Search, Explore Careers and Get Educated | Riley Guide*. Retrieved October 16, 2013, from http://www.rileyguide.com

institution: (n.d.). Academic | Legal Research for Students | LexisNexis®.*Business Solutions & Software for Legal, Education and Government | LexisNexis*. Retrieved October 18, 2013, from http://www.lexisnexis.com/en-us/products/lexisnexis-academic.page

It's our job to find your job. (n.d.). *It's our job to find your job*. Retrieved October 18, 2013, from http://www.jobster.com

Job Search | Jobwall.net. (n.d.). *Job Search | Jobwall.net*. Retrieved October 16, 2013, from http://jobwall.net

Job Search | one search. all jobs. Indeed.com. (n.d.). *Job Search | one search. all jobs. Indeed.com*. Retrieved October 16, 2013, from http://indeed.com

Job Search | View All Job Openings | Snagajob. (n.d.). *Job Search | View All Job Openings | Snagajob*. Retrieved October 18, 2013, from http://snagajob.com

Jobs - Careers - Employment - Job Search Engine | Simply Hired. (n.d.). *Jobs - Careers - Employment - Job Search Engine | Simply Hired*. Retrieved October 16, 2013, from http://simplyhired.com

Jobs & Job Search Advice, Employment & Careers | Careerbuilder.com. (n.d.). *Jobs & Job Search Advice, Employment & Careers | Careerbuilder.com*. Retrieved October 16, 2013, from http://www.careerbuilder.com/

Jobs, Employers, and Job Search Resources and Advice - Job-Hunt.org, @JobHuntOrg. (n.d.). *Jobs, Employers, and Job Search Resources and Advice - Job-Hunt.org, @JobHuntOrg*. Retrieved October 16, 2013, from http://www.job-hunt.org

jobs, s. t., productivity, c. s., & collaboration. (n.d.). Career Advice, Find a Job & Salary Trends - Wall Street Journal - Wsj.com. *Career Advice, Find a Job & Salary Trends - Wall Street Journal - Wsj.com*. Retrieved October 16, 2013, from http://www.careerjournal.com

Jobs2Careers: Job Search Engine, Search Jobs & Employment. (n.d.).*Jobs2Careers: Job Search Engine, Search Jobs & Employment*. Retrieved October 18, 2013, from http://www.jobs-to-careers.com

JobStar Guide to Salaries - 300+ Free Online Salary Surveys. (n.d.). *JobStar: Job Search Guide*. Retrieved October 16, 2013, from http://www.jobstar.org/tools/salary

JobStar Resume Guide -- Sample Resumes & Cover Letter Templates. (n.d.). *JobStar: Job Search Guide*. Retrieved October 18, 2013, from http://www.jobstar.org/tools/resume/index.php

Johnson, S. (2002). *Who moved my cheese? an a-mazing way to deal with change in your work and in your life* (Privately published ed., 12th ed.). New York: G.P. Putnam's Sons.

Kimeldorf, M. (n.d.). Amby's Site -- KIMELDORF: Portfolio Library ~~ Table of Contents. *Amby's Directory of Resources*. Retrieved October 18, 2013, from http://www.amby.com/kimeldorf/portfolio

Krannich, C. R., & Krannich, R. L. (2004). *Job interview tips for people with not-so-hot backgrounds: how to put red flags behind you to win the job*. Manassas Park, Va.: Impact Publications.

Manta. (n.d.). *Big finds from small businesses*. Retrieved October 16, 2013, from www.manta.com

Market Research, competitive intelligence, industry data, statistics, forecasts, US and global trends, corporate profiles, business information; reference books, executive mailing lists from Plunkett Research. (n.d.). *Market Research, competitive intelligence, industry data, statistics, forecasts, US and global trends, corporate profiles, business information; reference books, executive mailing lists from Plunkett Research*. Retrieved October 16, 2013, from http://www.plunkettresearch.com

Maxwell, J. C. (2002). *The 17 essential qualities of a team player: becoming the kind of person every team wants*. Nashville, Tenn.: T. Nelson.

Money. (n.d.). CNN Money. *CNN Money*. Retrieved October 17, 2013, from www.money.cnn.com

Month. (n.d.). U.S. Bureau of Labor Statistics. *U.S. Bureau of Labor Statistics.* Retrieved October 16, 2013, from http://bls.gov

My Space. (n.d.). *This is My Space.* Retrieved October 16, 2013, from https://myspace.com

My Workster. (n.d.). *My Workster.* Retrieved October 18, 2013, from http://www.myworkster.com

O*Net OnLine. (n.d.). *Welcome to your tool for career exploration and job analysis!* Retrieved October 16, 2013, from www.online.onetcenter.org

Payscale. (n.d.). *Salary Comparison.* Retrieved October 16, 2013, from www.payscale.com

People Search - Find People with MyLife. (n.d.). *People Search - Find People with MyLife.* Retrieved October 16, 2013, from http://www.mylife.com

Pinterest. (n.d.). *A few (million) of your favorite things.* Retrieved October 16, 2013, from https://www.pinterest.com

Pipl People Search. (n.d.). *The most comprehensive people search on the web.* Retrieved October 15, 2013, from https://pipl.com

Quintessential Careers. (n.d.). *College, Careers, and Jobs Guide.* Retrieved October 17, 2013, from www.quintcareers.com

Real Time Search - Social Mention. (n.d.).*Real Time Search - Social Mention.* Retrieved October 16, 2013, from http://socialmention.com

Realtor. (n.d.). *Where Home Happens.* Retrieved October 17, 2013, from www.realtor.com

Recent Job Openings | Posting Jobs | Graduate Jobs | Student Job Search. (n.d.). *Recent Job Openings | Posting Jobs | Graduate Jobs | Student Job Search.* Retrieved October 18, 2013, from http://www.educationlinked.com

ReferenceUSA. (n.d.). *ReferenceUSA.* Retrieved October 16, 2013, from http://www.referenceusa.com

Reliable Salary Data from Job Search Intelligence- Leading compensation data resource. (n.d.). *Reliable Salary Data from Job Search Intelligence- Leading compensation data resource.* Retrieved October 16, 2013, from http://www.jobsearchintelligence.com

Relocation Calculator - House Moving Costs and Resources | HomeFair.com. (n.d.). *Relocation Calculator - House Moving Costs and Resources | HomeFair.com.* Retrieved October 16, 2013, from http://www.homefair.com

Repa, B. K. (2010). *Your rights in the workplace* (9th ed.). Berkeley, CA: Nolo.

Retail Jobs | Retail Careers | Retail Resumes | Largest Retail Job Board. (n.d.). *Retail Jobs | Retail Careers | Retail Resumes | Largest Retail Job Board.* Retrieved October 18, 2013, from http://allretailjobs.com

SalaryExpert - Salary Survey, Compensation Data, Salaries, and Career Planning. (n.d.). *SalaryExpert - Salary Survey, Compensation Data, Salaries, and Career Planning.* Retrieved October 16, 2013, from http://www.salaryexpert.com

SEC.gov | Company Search Page. (n.d.).*U.S. Securities and Exchange Commission | Homepage.* Retrieved October 16, 2013, from http://www.sec.gov/edgar/searchedgar/ compan

Security Clearance Jobs - ClearanceJobs.com. (n.d.). *Security Clearance Jobs - ClearanceJobs. com.* Retrieved October 18, 2013, from http://www.clearancejobs.com

State Jobs - 50StateJobs.com. (n.d.).*State Jobs - 50StateJobs.com.* Retrieved October 18, 2013, from http://statejobs.com

Title, S. (n.d.). Dice.com - Job Search for Technology Professionals. *Dice.com - Job Search for Technology Professionals.* Retrieved October 16, 2013, from http://www.dice.com

TwitJobSearch.com - A Job Search Engine for Twitter. (n.d.). *TwitJobSearch.com - A Job Search Engine for Twitter.* Retrieved October 16, 2013, from http://www.twitjobsearch.com

Twitter. (n.d.). *Welcome to Twitter.* Retrieved October 16, 2013, from https://twitter.com

US Census Bureau. (n.d.). *Measuring America—People, Places, and Our Economy.* Retrieved October 16, 2013, from http://census.gov

US Department of Justice, Bureau of Justice Statistics, http://www.bjs.gov/content/pub/pdf/wv09.pdf

US.jobs - National Labor Exchange - USA Jobs Search Engine. (n.d.). *US.jobs - National Labor Exchange - USA Jobs Search Engine.* Retrieved October 18, 2013, from http://www.jobcentral.com

US.jobs - National Labor Exchange - USA Jobs Search Engine. (n.d.). *US.jobs - National Labor Exchange - USA Jobs Search Engine.* Retrieved October 18, 2013, from http://us.jobs

USAJOBS. (n.d.). *Working for America.* Retrieved October 17, 2013, from https://www.usajobs.gov

Vault.com - Get the inside scoop on companies, schools, internships, jobs and more. . (n.d.). *Vault.com - Get the inside scoop on companies, schools, internships, jobs and more. .* Retrieved October 16, 2013, from http://www.vault.com

VetJobs. (n.d.). *Veterans Make the Best Employees.* Retrieved October 17, 2013, from https://vetjobs.com

Wall Street Journal. (n.d.). Career Advice, Find a Job & Salary Trends - Wall Street Journal - Wsj.com. *The Wall Street Journal - Breaking News, Business, Financial and Economic News, World News & Video - Wall Street Journal - Wsj.com.* Retrieved October 16, 2013, from http://online.wsj.com/public/page/news-career-jobs.html

Welcome to Flickr - Photo Sharing. (n.d.).*Welcome to Flickr - Photo Sharing.* Retrieved October 16, 2013, from http://flickr.com

Welcome to Salary.com! - Salary.com. (n.d.). *Welcome to Salary.com! - Salary.com.* Retrieved October 16, 2013, from http://www.salary.com

Wetfeet. (n.d.). *Personalized, Insider Answers to Help You Get Your Dream Job.* Retrieved October 17, 2013, from www.wetfeet.com

World's Largest Professional Network | LinkedIn. (n.d.). *World's Largest Professional Network | LinkedIn.* Retrieved October 16, 2013, from http://linkedin.com

XING – The Professional Network | XING. (n.d.). *XING – The Professional Network| XING*. Retrieved October 16, 2013, from http://xing.com

Yate, Martin John. *Knock 'em dead: the ultimate job search guide, 2013*. Avon, Mass.: Adams Media, 2012.

You Version. (n.d.). *The New Bible.com*. Retrieved October 16, 2013, from https://www.bible.com/

YouTube. (n.d.). *YouTube*. Retrieved October 16, 2013, from http://www.youtube.com

CPSIA information can be obtained
at www.ICGtesting.com
Printed in the USA
LVOW02s1721010817
543423LV00002B/51/P